Amazing Stories®

TORONTO DISASTERS

Comments on other *Amazing Stories* from readers & reviewers

"You might call them the non-fiction response to Harlequin romances: easy to consume and potentially addictive."
Robert Martin, *The Chronicle Herald*

"Tightly written volumes filled with lots of wit and humour about famous and infamous Canadians."
Eric Shackleton, *The Globe and Mail*

"This is popular history as it should be... For this price, buy two and give one to a friend."
Terry Cook, a reader from Ottawa, on **Rebel Women**

"Stories are rich in description, and bristle with a clever, stylish realness."
Mark Weber, *Central Alberta Advisor,* on **Ghost Town Stories II**

"The resulting book is one readers will want to share with all the women in their lives."
Lynn Martel, *Rocky Mountain Outlook,* on **Women Explorers**

"[The books are] *long on plot and character and short on the sort of technical analysis that can be dreary for all but the most committed academic."*
Robert Martin, *The Chronicle Herald*

"A compelling read. Bertin ... has selected only the most intriguing tales, which she narrates with a wealth of detail."
Joyce Glasner, *New Brunswick Reader,* on **Strange Events**

"The heightened sense of drama and intrigue, combined with a good dose of human interest is what sets Amazing Stories *apart."*
Pamela Klaffke, *Calgary Herald*

TORONTO DISASTERS

Devastation and Tragedies that Made the Headlines

HISTORY/HUMAN INTEREST

by Kathlyn Horibe

This book is dedicated to my son, Mike.

PUBLISHED BY ALTITUDE PUBLISHING CANADA LTD.
1500 Railway Avenue, Canmore, Alberta T1W 1P6
www.altitudepublishing.com
www.amazingstories.ca
1-800-957-6888

Extreme care has been taken to ensure that all information presented in this book is accurate and up to date. Neither the author nor the publisher can be held responsible for any errors.

Publisher	Stephen Hutchings
Series Editor	Diana Marshall
Editors	Joan Dixon and Laurie Drukier
Cover and Layout	Bryan Pezzi

We acknowledge the financial support of the Government of Canada through the Book Publishing Industry Development Program (BPIDP) for our publishing activities.

Altitude GreenTree Program
Altitude Publishing will plant twice as many trees as were used in the manufacturing of this product.

National Library of Canada Cataloguing in Publication Data

Horibe, Kathlyn
Toronto disasters / Kathlyn Horibe.

(Amazing stories)
ISBN 1-55439-032-X

1. Natural disasters--Ontario--Toronto--History.
2. Disasters--Ontario--Toronto--History. 3. Toronto (Ont.)--History.
I. Title. II. Series: Amazing stories (Canmore, Alta.)

FC3097.4.H67 2006   971.3'541   C2006-902035-3

Amazing Stories® is a registered trademark of Altitude Publishing Canada Ltd.

Printed and bound in Canada by Friesens
2 4 6 8 9 7 5 3 1

Contents

Prologue

Volunteer firefighter Bryan Mitchell will never forget Hurricane Hazel's night of devastation.

"On October 15, 1954, I was on duty at the fire station in Etobicoke and all day long we received calls about flooded basements. Around 4 o'clock, I took another call. The railroad underpass at Kipling Avenue had flooded, trapping a truck. I suggested they call a nearby station for their aerial trucks because our station didn't have any. Moments later, they phoned back — their aerials had gone into the ditch because of the rain.

"I dispatched a ladder truck. By the time the firefighters arrived, water was up to the truck's cab. Four cars were also covered. The water kept going up and up and up. The firemen threw ropes across to the drivers, who had climbed onto the roofs of the higher vehicles. They tied themselves on and they were pulled to higher ground an hour later. Everyone went home and the rain seemed to abate a bit."

The crisis had been averted, or so he thought. Later the same day ...

"Around 9 p.m., the rain started pouring down again. The power went off and the winds were strong with a lot of lightning strikes. I got a house fire all cleared up and I drove home around 11:30 p.m. I couldn't see where the road ended and the ditches started because the rain was coming down so hard. Cars were in ditches everywhere along the two-lane highway.

"I tried to get some sleep but the hotline phone kept ringing. My father was chief of the department and the phone was connected to our house. But he was away at a firemen's convention in the U.S.

"Then a call came in about a flooded dance hall up in Thistletown. Then a second call came in about a man stuck on the Phillips Road Bridge. Both sides of the approaches were washed away. I said I would drop by to see what's happening on my way to Thistletown."

Bryan Mitchell hadn't planned on what happened next.

Chapter 1
The Great
Fire of 1904

On April 12, 1904, Fire Chief John Thompson appeared before the city's Board of Control. In his presentation, he warned that the Toronto fire department had serious weaknesses. The existing water hydrant system was inadequate, and cities smaller than Toronto had more steam-powered fire engines. "We are taking more and more risks every year," he said. "We are running in wonderful luck. Some day we will have two or three alarms at once and the department will only answer one and the other fires will be eating up valuable property. The need of a new system is imperative."

By this time, firefighting equipment in Canada had attained a certain level of sophistication. Human chain bucket brigades had evolved into hydrant systems, rescue ladders, steam-powered fire engines, and portable, pressurized fire extinguishers capable of shooting a stream of water 62 metres high.

Toronto's population was 200,000 in 1904 and as the centre of import and export for Ontario, it was an important commercial centre for Canada, second only to Montreal. A jumble of warehouses and buildings housing commercial, financial, and manufacturing businesses crowded the downtown mercantile district. Skyscrapers of four to six storeys dotted the burgeoning skyline.

Notwithstanding, the fire chief's request of $35,000 to improve fire protection was denied.

A week later, on April 19, 1904, night watchman T. H. Johnson turned onto Wellington Street West from Bay Street on his usual rounds. As the stinging snow whipped around the corner, he burrowed deeper into his coat. The temperature was –4 degrees Celsius, unseasonably cold for that time of year. Then the watchman smelled smoke. He hurried down the alley that ran along the west side of the E. & S. Currie necktie factory (where the Toronto-Dominion Centre now sits).

"All of a sudden, I heard a roaring sound," he said. "I rushed to the back of the building and there I saw a column of smoke shooting up the elevator shaft." He raced to Bay Street, slipping on the ice in his haste, and rang the fire alarm of Box 12 on the corner of King Street. Although the telephone was now common, the fire alarm box on street corners remained the main means of sounding an alarm. "When I got back from turning in the alarm," he said, "the flames completely enveloped the rear end of the Currie building and was fast eating into the front." It was 8:04 p.m.

Around the same time, Constable William Lannin also spied smoke. At the corner of York and Front Streets, he turned in an alarm at Box 7.

The almost simultaneous alarms sounded at the Lombard Street Fire Hall a few blocks away. Without wasting any time, the firefighters jumped onto the fire wagons and the horses thundered out of the station, bells clanging. Horses had replaced humans to transport fire equipment by the turn of the century and some fire departments even employed career firefighters.

"By the time the fire reels reached the spot," watchman Johnson said, "the flames had started to lap the side of Ansley's, the furriers to the east of Currie's ..."

Fire Chief Thompson himself arrived to take charge. At the scene, along with the firefighters, were seven hose wagons, three steam engines, two chemical engines, aerial trucks, hook and ladder trucks, a salvage wagon, and a water tower.

As Chief Thompson well knew, development in the commercial district had not kept pace with fire protection and building codes. The brick and stone exteriors of the buildings, which hid substantial quantities of combustible materials, presented a false sense of security. The simple wood joist construction had open floor plans, vertical elevator shafts, and stairways with no firebreaks between buildings. Ornate wooden cornices and dormers decorated the exterior windows and tar covered the flat roofs. The automatic sprinkler system had been around for 20 years as well as its exterior adaptation — the water curtain. However, only three commercial buildings in Toronto's business district had installed them.

By the time the chief arrived, the fire had blazed through all four floors of the Currie clothing factory and warehouse. Open elevator shafts had funnelled the fire from the very bottom to the very top of the brick and wood joist structure. Chief Thompson positioned his men in the front and rear of the building and they immediately started dousing the flames with five streams of water.

To prevent the fire from spreading to the building across the alley, Chief Thompson and four firemen forced their way into hat manufacturer Gillespie-Ansley. From its six-storey roof, they planned to flood water onto Currie's. But when they reached the third storey, they were forced back. Fanned by the wind, flames had licked their way through the wooden window frames. Smoke filled the floor. Without any lanterns, they could not find the stairway down. Smoke burning their eyes, they lurched to a window, shattered the glass, and shouted for help.

Fortunately, the firemen outside heard their cries. They tried to prop up a ladder against the building but it fell short. One of the trapped firefighters tossed a rope outside the window. With a hose secured to it, the men slid down to safety. Chief Thompson, the last to leave, slipped. "I slid down very fast, my right leg striking the asphalt pavement first with great force," he said.

An ambulance transported the fire chief to Emergency Hospital where he was diagnosed with a broken leg and torn ligaments. Fraught with worry, he was later transported to his home to recuperate; the hospital was just too close to the fire for him to feel comfortable. It was a critical moment to lose the chief and his accident cost vital time in fighting the spreading fire.

By the time his replacement, Deputy Chief John Noble, arrived, the combustible materials inside the Gillespie-Ansley building had burst into flames, engulfing the entire structure. The deputy chief rang in a general alarm at 8:51 p.m., less than an hour after the first alarm.

Every available fireman from Toronto's 15 fire halls raced through the downtown core. The sight of horses at full gallop pulling steam engines, ladder trucks, hose wagons, and hook and ladder sleighs also drew curious spectators.

The blaze fanned out in two directions. From Currie's, it spread west along Wellington and headed north. From the Gillespie-Ansley building, strong gusts blew the flames east to the woollen goods warehouse of Dignum and Moneypenny. At the intersection of Bay and Wellington Streets, firemen set up the tall cannon-like water tower and directed its hose at the roof and the upper floors. Concerned about the flames vaulting east, Deputy Chief Noble mounted a defence of 20 hose streams on Bay Street, but weak water pressure hampered efforts.

As the fire chief had warned the city's board, fire hydrants in the heavily congested business district had narrow branch lines 15 or 30 centimetres wide, which were fed principally from a 61-centimetre feeder along Front Street. Water pressure reached only 80 pounds per square inch compared to Buffalo's and Detroit's 350 pounds per square inch. In addition, the Rosehill reservoir supplied water for both the fire hydrants and city homes.

Toronto's entire fire squadron of 196 men now battled the stubborn flames on three separate blocks. But Mother Nature hindered their efforts. Gusting 48-kilometre-per-hour winds from the northwest blew the firefighters off their feet and hampered them from aiming the hoses into the storm. The wind cut the streams of water in two and blew the spray back, coating their faces and hands with ice.

Electricity poles, lined up like soldiers along the front of the buildings, prevented the firemen from propping up ladders against the façades. Fallen utility poles littered the streets along with a maze of electricity, telephone, and telegraph wires. Throughout the night, the men ducked tumbling poles and scrambled over frozen wires scattered along the streets.

By now, more Torontonians had been alerted about the blaze and some business owners had panicked. The firemen then had to contend with express wagons weaving in and out of the business district, their drivers rescuing merchandise from threatened buildings. Slipping on the icy streets, horses stumbled and lost their footing. Businessmen and shop owners frantically searched through their commercial establishments looking for important documents.

Shortly after 9 p.m., the situation worsened. The front wall of a building crashed onto Bay Street sending a wall of fire toward the *Evening Telegram* building. The plate glass windows of the daily newspaper office shattered. Thick smoke poured in but the rudimentary automatic sprinkler system failed to activate.

With wet towels protecting their heads, *Telegram* employees stayed and helped fight the fire for over two hours. They hooked up fire hoses to the hydrant on the roof and from every window directed the streams at the wooden cornices of the building. The iron shutters on the windows helped to prevent the flames from eating at the building. Their valiant efforts saved the building — much to the appreciation of *Telegram* publisher John Ross Robertson. He later rewarded his employees with sizeable bonuses.

"The *Telegram* building was a difficult one to save," Deputy Chief Noble said, "but we knew that if we didn't save it, a great amount of valuable property would be destroyed to the east." The newspaper building provided the firebreak the firefighters needed for the northern perimeter. The fire was now prevented from spreading up Bay Street to King, Queen and Yonge Streets, and the new City Hall.

However, the inferno continued to devour building after building, illuminating the night sky with flames shooting 30 metres into the air. By the time Toronto Mayor Thomas Urquhart arrived at 11:30 p.m., the fire had gutted the entire area west of Bay from Wellington to Front Street. Deputy Chief Noble requested more help and the mayor called for reinforcements. Fifteen minutes later, 26 firemen arrived from Kew Beach, Toronto Junction, and East Toronto, along with 152-metre hoses. Toronto's suburban municipalities as well as Hamilton, Buffalo, Brantford, Niagara Falls, London, and Peterborough also pledged to help. When 10 Hamilton firemen arrived with over 425 metres of hose, spectators roared with approval.

Meanwhile, the fight was on to save the luxurious Queen's Hotel between Wellington and Front, the site of today's Fairmont Royal York Hotel. In addition to the usual tourists, guests at the venerated hotel included many prominent members of parliament — since the provincial legislature was in session.

When the printing and bookbinding company, Warwick Brothers & Rutter, located next to the hotel, caught on fire, District Chief Frank Smith organized his men and the Hamilton firefighters on the hotel roof. Though a 18-metre garden protected the Queen's Hotel from the burning building, the wind was intense. Icy blasts atop the building froze the hoses of the firefighters.

Fortunately, inside the hotel, manager Henry Winnett

led an amateur fire brigade, made up of many of his distin-
guished guests. Mrs. Winnett, the manager's wife, instructed
the staff to remove blankets from hotel beds and soak them
in water. The wet bedspreads were then suspended from the
windows to keep the wood from catching fire. Maids, cooks,
and bellboys stood precariously on tables and chairs to
pour buckets of water over the suspended blankets. Due to
their efforts, only minor scorches marred the exterior of the
Queen's Hotel.

But as the night wore on, the situation became more
desperate. Mayor Urquhart agreed to use dynamite to create
a firebreak, although Chief City Architect Robert McCallum
cautioned that explosives could spread the fire. Military engineers from the Stanley Barracks Garrison were called in, but,
in the end, no dynamite could be found.

Instead, the troops were put to work helping police control the growing crowd. Thousands of people now thronged
Front Street, braving the freezing temperatures and jostling
for ringside views to the fiery spectacle. They leaned out of
windowsills or gathered on steps. Some were clad in fur coats,
others were inadequately clothed. Many munched on sandwiches and kept warm by drinking coffee. When they saw a
wall about to collapse, they shouted warnings. Whenever the
firemen defeated disaster, they cheered them on.

Many of these helpful bystanders were injured. Even
from a distance of 90 metres, the heat was intense. Chunks of
burning wood and glass shards cluttered streets. Throughout

the night, Emergency Hospital admitted more injured spectators and wounded firemen. Many firefighters were momentarily blinded with the intense heat and smoke painfully inflaming their eyes. After treatment, they went back to the fire only to return to the hospital again and again until practically blinded. Some had to be sent home to recover. The cold exhausted others. The injuries were so numerous that a line of stricken men snaked down the hospital corridor with the doctors hard pressed to keep up.

South of Front Street, flames fuelled by the wind ate away at the factories. At the Eckardt Casket Company, employees tried to save a half dozen hearses with only one skittish horse. A few spectators came to their rescue and lugged the hearses out of the danger area. At the Hendrie Cartage Company, pandemonium ensued when grooms tried to remove the horses from the stables. They grabbed any harnesses they could find and fitted them onto the nervous horses.

On the waterfront, Captain Malone of the Richelieu and Ontario Company spent the night protecting the harbour. Thanks to him and the men under his direction, the wharves were saved. "The sparks were coming so thick," he said, "and it seemed so imminent that the boats moored to the wharves would be burnt that we simply cut their lines and allowed them to drift out into the bay."

The tugboat *Clark* steamed out and towed the drifting boats to safe anchorage. Not so lucky, the steamer *Owen Sound* remained tied to the dock and caught on fire in many places. Fortunately, the drifting sparks did not reach the larger steamers *Toronto* and *Kingston,* moored at the foot of Bay Street, but their crew stood at the ready with buckets and hoses in case they did.

About 11:30 p.m., fire struck the McLaughlin flour mills on Esplanade Street and every business west of it. Cinders fell like snowflakes. Fuelled by the gale, the fire hung over the railway tracks below Esplanade, threatening piles of lumber at Cobban Manufacturing.

At midnight, the uncontrollable inferno swept along the south side of Front Street. Rivers of water flowed down both sides of the street from the dozens of hoses. The intense heat almost caused several firefighters to pass out. When the fire reached the gun and ammunition warehouse of H.S. Howland Sons, hundred of thousands of cartridges detonated. "What with the noise ... and the roaring of the fire, you could not hear yourself shout," an eyewitness said.

By 3 a.m., when the flames reached the Kilgour Brothers' paper box factory on Wellington, the fire had made a complete U-turn from its place of origin. Fortunately, the Kilgour's water curtain on the south side provided a firebreak. To keep the fire from spreading to Yonge Street, Chief Noble rallied his men. "We have got to stop that fire at that Minerva building." If they stopped the fire there, the Bank of Montreal, which fronted Yonge Street, would not be imperilled.

When the inferno was still a distance away, Mr. W. Wingfield, the company engineer at the Minerva building, had hurried down to organize his staff. Wielding company hoses and fire extinguishers, the employees fought the fire from the icy rooftop. Firemen positioned their hoses outside the building. Staff from the Salada Tea Company on Yonge Street, next to the Bank of Montreal, also streamed their company's equipment onto the Minerva windows.

With hoses in position, the firefighters waited for the water to gush out. Icicles formed on their eyebrows. Minutes passed with the hoses still limp and the fire advancing. Then with a burst, the water surged out. Despite their efforts, however, the entire top floor caught fire and the firefighters disappeared from sight for 10 anxious minutes. Suddenly they reappeared. Despite pleas from the crowd to come down, they returned for an all-out attack. Just as the sun rose, the fire at the Minerva was extinguished.

Deputy Chief Noble exclaimed: "There! We have her beaten now! I tell you it was a mighty tight struggle all the way."

But on the south side, the inferno had reached the rear of McMahon, Broadfield, a wholesale crockery establishment on Front Street and was coursing across the lane to the Customs examining warehouse south of the Customs House on Yonge Street. The fight was still on to stop the fire from reaching Yonge Street. For two steady hours, firefighters kept their hoses aimed at both buildings with only a vacant 15-metre lot separating them. Then the McMahon roof caved in and all seemed lost.

District Chief Smedley directed five of his men to get in closer, but the McMahon's east and south walls began to waver. "Run for your lives," shouted Police Constable Dent. Hundreds of bricks clattered to the ground in a deafening roar. When the clouds of orange smoke cleared, heads were anxiously counted. All the men were safe.

The collapse of the McMahon stopped the fire in its tracks, and prevented its spreading to Yonge Street. With their final stand, the firemen saved the Customs House and the buildings housing the Bank of Montreal, the Salada Tea Company, the Bank of Hamilton, and other property north of Wellington Street.

It was 4:30 a.m. The fire had roared with extraordinary ferocity for more than eight hours but miraculously no one had been killed. Weeks after, the Great Fire claimed its only casualty. John Croft died while dynamiting what was left of the Gage Building on Front Street where the Royal Bank tower exists today.

More than 7.7 hectares of prime real estate from south of Wellington Street to Esplanade and east of Lorne to Yonge had been reduced to scorched rubble. The losses were estimated at $10.5 million in 1904 dollars. The fire had destroyed 98 buildings and nearly 220 businesses. Mr. W. J. Hill, one of the largest builders in the province, estimated it would take five years to rebuild.

The destruction of the building housing the provincial government printer, Warwick Brothers & Rutter, left 2,500

After the fire, only skeletal ruins of buildings remained

pages of type in a "mass of molten lead." These included session journals, statutes, reports, bills passed or about to be
passed at the current sitting of the House. Though some safes
and vaults had protected valuable documents, companies
with no copies of duplicate receipts lost hundreds of thousands of dollars. Insurance covered only about 80 percent of
the damage.

Many of the businesses set up again in temporary
lodgings. Between 5,000 and 6,000 people, mainly women,
lost their jobs. The day after the fire, some arrived for work

at 8 o'clock as usual, unaware their place of employment had been gutted. Some of the more fortunate men found employment clearing away the debris but night watchman T. H. Johnson lost his job. "All the buildings that I have been watching for so long are all gone," he said.

Chief Thompson finally received the funds to hire more men and buy equipment such as large capacity steam engines. A system of high-pressure water mains with 300 pounds per inch of pressure was installed in Toronto. The city passed a bylaw for more stringent building standards.

The next large fire in Toronto occurred 75 years later in May 1979. The old Eaton department store on Yonge Street and a number of its warehouses were under demolition when fire struck. The flames, again whipped by the wind, spread to other buildings including Old City Hall. This time, powerful motor pumpers supplied the water to squelch the fire before any major damage was done.

Chapter 2
SS *Noronic*

On September 17, 1949, around 4 p.m., the largest cruise ship on the Great Lakes slipped into her Pier 9 berth at the foot of Yonge Street. On board the *Noronic*, the flagship of Canada Steamship Lines, were 524 passengers, the majority holidaying Americans from Cleveland, and a crew of 171.

The *Noronic* epitomized luxury. Towering five decks high, and longer than a football field, "the Queen of the Inland Seas" boasted carved staircases, floor-to-ceiling windows in the dining room and long promenade decks. Amenities included library and music rooms, a barber shop, a beauty parlour, a children's playroom, buffet bars, and a daily published newspaper. On-board activities for the passengers ranged from bingo and euchre tournaments to gala costume balls.

SS Noronic

The special late-summer luxury cruise was scheduled to layover the night in Toronto before continuing on to Canada's Thousand Islands. In spite of the many amenities aboard, most of the passengers eagerly disembarked after the eight-hour journey to tour the city. The evening a balmy 15 degrees Celsius, Captain William Taylor also left his ship, leaving only 16 crew on duty.

It was usually the special officer's responsibility to conduct a thorough hourly inspection of the ship, punching the clock with each deck's key. But neither of the special officers was on duty that night. Coming on watch at midnight, the two wheelsmen, James Donaldson and Everett Pepper, had been ordered instead to conduct the fire patrol of the ship. "I was only on the boat for three months," said James, then 21 years old. "That was the first time I went through the meat locker, down in all the holes, in the galley, up and down every hall, punching this clock. The patrol took about half an hour."

After concluding the inspection, the two wheelsman then stood on the gangplank to welcome the returning passengers. The *Noronic* was secured to the dock on the starboard side. To get to their cabins, the passengers embarked through the starboard gangplank. Passenger decks on the *Noronic* were labelled A, B, C, and D with the only entry and exit located on E, the lowest deck.

While the majority of the crew remained ashore, the captain came back on board around 1 a.m. and went up to his room on the top deck. By then, most of the passengers were also back on board.

After the night on the town with his wife, sleep was still eluding passenger Don Church when he smelled smoke. Familiar with the deadly consequences of fire, the insurance appraiser dashed starboard along C deck toward a smoky haze. He traced the burning smell to a linen closet off the port corridor. Smoke spiralled from inside the door. He gingerly touched the handle and heard a crackling noise. He tugged at the door but the room was locked.

Running toward the social hall amidships, he yelled, "Fire! Fire!" almost colliding with Garth O'Neill, the head bus boy. Both men ran back to the fire where Garth fumbled with a ring of keys trying to open the door. Discovering he didn't have the right one, he scampered down the aft stairway to the steward's office on D deck. He grabbed the key, sprinted back up the stairwell, and raced past the fire to the vessel's stern to retrieve the extinguisher from the lounge.

By now, another passenger, Cleveland businessman Ben Kosman had also smelled smoke. When he saw bus boys hustling along the passageway with fire extinguishers, he followed them. "They opened the door to the room," Ben later said. "They shouldn't have done that. The flames roared out." As soon as air entered the closet, the fire fanned out onto the deck. Flames also licked the ceiling. "They couldn't, or didn't, close the door again," Ben said.

In the C deck parlour amidships, Sanford and Harriet

Newman were also still up, playing cards with friends when they heard someone screaming, "Fire!" Flinging his cards onto the table, Sanford opened the parlour door and raced along the corridor toward the acrid smell. He discovered two bus boys failing to quell the fire with extinguishers. Flames engulfed the cherry and oak walls and ceilings, dotingly maintained for 36 years with layers of paint and lemon oil. Choked by the fumes, Sanford dashed back to the parlour to warn his wife and friends.

Realizing the extinguishers were ineffective, Don ran to the hose station, unrolled the fire hose, and returned, pulling it behind him. When he opened the hydrant valve, only a trickle of water spewed out. When he realized the fire might not be contained, he rushed to his stateroom on D deck to rouse his family.

Meanwhile, bus boy O'Neill ran off to sound the fire alarm box in the social hall. He smashed the glass with a hammer so the bell would clang in the officers' quarters on A deck. Then he dashed to get help. He ran into the two wheelsmen still on the E deck gangplank, covering other duties. One of them was supposed to be in the pilot house ready to activate the klaxon horn to signal fire to passengers.

"When the bus boy said 'There's a fire,'" James remembered, "I went up to A deck and told the captain who was getting ready for bed. He said something to me but I didn't understand what he said. I went to get the first mate out of bed and told him about the fire."

First Mate Gerry Wood immediately spied smoke coming from the starboard side. It was only eight minutes after the fire had begun and half the decks were ablaze. He ran to the wheelhouse to sound the ship's warning system. The horn seized, and rather than a series of blasts, it released a bone-chilling shriek.

Fire had always been a menace to ships, on the water especially, but also near shore. In 1945, *Noronic*'s sister ship, the *Hamonic,* had burned while moored at Point Edward, Ontario, at a dock that had caught fire. The crew had been unable to quickly sail her away.

The *Noronic* had sailed more than a 1,000 voyages safely — despite not conforming to Canadian fire protection regulations. Built in 1913, the "Norey" was exempt from regulations implemented in 1939. Though she was constructed of iron and steel, wooden planks covered her steel decks and exotic woods covered the ceilings and interiors, which were maintained with combustible paints. Wooden partitions subdivided most of the ship, including stairwells, decks, and cabins. With no vertical fire bulkheads throughout the vessel, fire could sweep through its long passageways with explosive force.

James continued trying to wake the passengers by hollering and banging on porthole windows. "But a lot of them were drunk at 1:30 in the morning," he said. When the wheelsmen had conducted their earlier rounds, they'd had to decline many invitations to join passengers for drinks.

He rushed to his room to alert the other crew members

and then returned to pounding on portholes. "From the time the bus boy told me there was a fire and I went up to the captain and around a little bit, the whole damn thing was on fire just about," James said. His frantic tour had taken 20 minutes.

Passenger Emil Dahlke of Hazel Park, Michigan, awoke to the sound of banging. Yanking open the cabin door, he encountered a blast of heat and flames. He and his wife ran to their stateroom window and managed to push out the screen. "A deckhand grabbed our shoulders and pulled us through the small porthole," Emil said.

Clad only in their night clothes, Victor and Cecile Stubbings rushed out onto D deck after waking up to a woman shouting, 'There's a bad fire!' "The scene that met our eyes was a living nightmare," Victor said. "It was like a reproduction of Hades. Burning embers were falling from the upper decks. Half-clad women of all ages dashed down the deck. An hysterical woman ran up and down, tearing at her hair."

All the commotion woke up passenger Josephine Kerr, travelling with her brother's family. When she saw the leaping flames in the corridor, she roused her two nieces, Kathleen and Barbara, and raced to her brother's cabin. She pounded on his door trying to wake him, her sister-in-law and eight-year-old nephew. No one answered. Thinking they were already safe, she grabbed her nieces by the hand and searched for a way to get off the ship. Dense black smoke forced them to the bow of the ship. There, 11-year-old Kathleen grabbed a red hot steel cable and slid down it, burning her hands and legs. She was then knocked into the water nine metres below by a man scrambling down the cable after her. Passenger Art Alves sat Kathleen's six-year-old sister, Barbara, on his shoulders and climbed down a rope. Josephine jumped, hit the anchor cable, and landed in the water.

On Pier 9, night watchman Harper had heard a noise coming from the *Noronic*. He gasped when he saw flames and smoke raging from the portholes between B and C decks. He ran to his office and dialled the operator who put him through to the fire department. The first alarm sounded at the Adelaide Street Fire Hall at 2:38 a.m. A disembarked passenger then rushed into watchman Harper's office appealing for an ambulance. Back on the phone, Harper told police to send as many ambulances and doctors as possible.

Firefighters raced to the fire with a pumper, a hose wagon, a high-pressure unit, and an aerial truck. One minute later, a fire boat streamed at full throttle toward the inferno. "As we went down Yonge Street and coming up on Queen's Quay," said firefighter Thomas Benson, "we could see the boat was a mass of flames."

District Fire Chief Jim Stevens radioed in a second alarm at 2:41 a.m. By the time the first trucks pulled up to Pier 9, flames enveloped the top three decks of the ship, silhouetting the desperate passengers against the night sky. He called in a third alarm.

On board the burning *Noronic,* some passengers wandered around in a daze. "'How do we get off? How do we get off?'" James reported them saying. "They hadn't been on the boat long enough to really be familiar with it and the hallways were long and all the lights were out." In addition, fire drills had not been conducted nor had passengers been instructed on evacuation procedures. Trapped on the upper decks, many were forced to jump into the black murky harbour water.

In addition to James, other crew were busy alerting the passengers. Bus boy Jack Brough smashed an axe through windows on the promenade deck to rescue passengers trapped in their cabins. "I found one woman lying face down in water that came up a foot [30.5 cm] on the cabin floor."

"Hundreds were rushing around the ship screaming and crying out for their relatives and friends," passenger Emil Dahlke said. "Women were knocked down in the struggle. All I could think of was getting my wife from the inferno. We ran to the side of the ship and I slid down a hawser [rope] with my wife on my shoulder."

More fire trucks and ambulances converged on the pier. Curious onlookers and a few late returning passengers watched as firefighters quickly hooked up hoses to the hydrants. Then they unrolled more hoses and tossed them into the harbour to suck up the water. "It was chaotic," firefighter Thomas Benson said. "Everything was happening all at once." To add to the din, the ship's horn kept blowing a strange and eerie sound throughout the night until the steam ran out.

Aerial ladder No. 5 was set up near the *Noronic*'s bow. Before the 26-metre wooden ladder could be properly secured to B deck, a desperate woman scrambled on, followed by several men. Partway down, she slipped and the men jammed into her. Their combined weight snapped the ladder in two, flinging them all into the harbour's cold water. Aerial No. 1 extended its 30-metre ladder to C deck. Firefighters worked at bracing it with hand ladders so it would not collapse. Then passengers scrambled onto it.

"Someone had thrown a rope ladder over the dockside, but it was all tangled up," said Sylvia Carpenter of Detroit, Michigan, who tried to help fellow passengers off the blazing vessel. "Then a rope was tossed over the rail. I put a hitch knot in it to hold it to a stanchion. As I did, three men pushed in front of me and shoved some screaming women out of the way. The men went down the rope."

Firefighter Thomas Benson and four other squad members rescued the people in the harbour. "It was tough getting them out," he said. "Hand ladders were pulled down by the weight of the people trying to climb up. In one instance, we tried pulling a guy out on a ladder, but he fell back in." They began using ropes instead, which worked much better.

Then the fireboat appeared on the scene and secured itself to the *Noronic*'s port bow. At dangerously close range, it drenched flames from a turret nozzle and two single lines while crew members jumped into the water to retrieve passengers. "The fireboat was able to pull a few out," Thomas

said, "but some were floating face down with their life pre-
servers on and were obviously dead."

Ross Leitch, the owner of a water taxi, arrived with two
of his friends to help. Dodging falling bodies, they started
pulling passengers into the boat. "I saw people dropping off
the *Noronic* like flies," he said. "As soon as they saw my boat,
they started to jump from the first deck onto my boat and
into the water. Some of them landed on the roof of my cabin
and broke through it. There was blood all over my boat. I
think I carried about 150 people to safety." Another Good
Samaritan, Donald Willamson, rescued 20 passengers in two
hours with a raft he found near the vessel's stern.

The *Noronic* had 14 lifeboats, seven on each side of
the vessel. Each could hold 38 people. A lifeboat drill was
conducted every time the crew arrived in Duluth, Wisconsin,
where the ship usually ended its summer run. However, the
drill was always conducted on the *port* side.

Lowering a lifeboat on the *starboard* side, wheelsman
James Donaldson had one of the other crew help him to
push it out. "There were a couple of knots in the lifeboat on
the starboard side," he said, "and I couldn't get them out." He
tried to control the speed of the lifeboat's descent onto the
dock with the brake. "Usually one fellow stands at the edge to
guide you. Well, he took off and I didn't know how far down
it was." Three-quarters of the way down, the lifeboat with 10
people hit the dock with a thud.

Suddenly, a ball of flame blazed out of the side of the

ship near James. He decided it was time to get off the ship. Fifteen metres in the air, hand over hand, he crawled along a one-and-a-half metre wide davit, which secured the lifeboat rope, to reach the line that had lowered the lifeboat. Then he slid down onto the dock.

As soon as James landed safely on the pier, someone thrust a hose into his hands. The wheelsman directed the hose at the stern of the vessel but the heat was so intense, water vaporized before reaching the ship. When he was relieved an hour and a half later, he went up to the bow. "Holy mackerel, you could see the fire going up sky high. You could hear dishes breaking, windows breaking." The *Noronic*'s decks had started to buckle and cave into one another and the metal hull had turned white hot.

Around 3:30 a.m. — about an hour after the fire started — the 6,264-tonne *Noronic* began to list precariously against the pier from large quantities of water swamping its hull. Deputy Chief Herd ordered his men and the fireboat to retreat. After a short time, the ship finally righted herself. By the time they wrestled the blaze under control at 5 a.m., more than 6.4 million litres of water had been dumped on the burning hull. But it was still too hot to board.

"We got aboard at daylight," firefighter Thomas Benson said, "and there were bodies everywhere. Some, but not all, were cremated, with just a skull or backbone remaining." Firefighters filled the tarps with body after body and carried them to a temporary morgue on the pier. But the charred

SS Noronic

Only the table supports remain in the charred wreckage
of what was once the dining room of the SS *Noronic*
after the disaster that claimed more than 100 lives.

remains became too numerous and a larger facility was
organized at the horticultural building on the grounds of the
Canadian National Exhibition.

The official death toll from the fire on the *Noronic* was
104 dead and 14 missing. None of the crew perished. Bus boy
O'Neill had fled the ship because of poor training. Insurance
appraiser Church and his family also left the ship without
waking other passengers. Sanford and Harriet Newman and
their card-playing friends from Cleveland survived, likely
because they had been able to act quickly. Eleven-year-old
Kathleen Kerr swam to shore safely and was reunited with

her sister and aunt. Her parents and her brother did not survive the fire.

The federal inquiry established by the House of Commons never determined the actual cause of the fire but the *Noronic*'s fire protection measures were deemed insufficient and the training of its officers and crew inadequate. Also at fault was the design and construction of the 36-year-old ship, which lacked fire resistant bulkheads and sufficient fire exits. In addition, the master and the ship's owners had failed to consider the possibility of fire occurring in harbour and no plan had been activated to evacuate the passengers once the fire had started. The victims' families received almost $3 million from Canada Steamship Lines and Captain Taylor was suspended for one year for failing to take effective command of the fire emergency.

As a result of the inquiry, strict regulations for both new and existing ships were enacted in 1950, the beginning of a new phase in Canadian marine standards for protection against fire. A number of Canadian passenger ships were either modified or taken out of service as a result, ending an era in decadent cruising on the Great Lakes.

About a month later, the *Noronic,* which had settled to the bottom of the harbour, was refloated and towed to a scrap yard in Hamilton, Ontario. A memorial to the victims of the tragic fire was established at Mount Pleasant Cemetery. Today, the Westin Harbour Castle Hotel sits on the site of Toronto's Pier 9.

Chapter 3
Hurricane Hazel

ometime after supper on October 15, 1954, Jim Crawford poked his younger brother Patrick. "Let's go over to the Humber," the 24-year-old off-duty police officer said, "I think we can make heroes of ourselves tonight."

Above average rainfall had saturated the Toronto area for two weeks. Now, after three straight days of rain, Jim knew from his familiarity with the area that "it was going to be quite a catastrophe that night because the water was rising higher and higher all the time."

Hurricane Hazel was responsible for the downpour. After her swath of destruction in Haiti and South Carolina, she had picked up speed, fuelled by a cold front from the Rockies, and moved north through North Carolina, Virginia,

Washington, D.C., and Maryland with 200- to 240-kilometre-per-hour winds and record rainfall. Meteorologists predicted more rain that night for the Toronto area. But they also presumed the Allegheny mountain range would weaken Hazel's intensity.

The Crawford brothers set out in Jim's pride and joy, his 1950 Pontiac. Rivers of rain streamed down the windshield, hampering their visibility and the car swayed violently from the gale force winds. At Jane Street and Wilson Avenue, a dip in the road immersed their car up to the hood. "I thought the water would clonk the spark plugs out," Jim said, "but we coasted very slowly through the intersection."

They drove south to Weston Road in the city's west end and turned onto the "flats," an apt name for the area on the east side of the Humber River, which snaked south from Woodbridge through the Toronto suburb of Etobicoke toward Lake Ontario. Jim parked at a safe distance from the swiftly moving river and the brothers walked down to the shoreline. They joined nearly 100 other people, including police officers and firefighters, who had gathered on the banks to witness an incredible sight.

The cresting river had torn about 50 homes from their foundations and set them afloat.

"Nobody could get out to the houses because of the heavy, heavy flow of the water," Jim said. "There was debris and cows, stumps of trees, and telephone poles floating down the Humber toward Lake Ontario. I just couldn't believe how high the Humber had risen around Fair Glen Crescent. It was as high as the telephone wires. People were literally screaming for their lives because they couldn't get out of their houses. Some were on second-floor porches, some were on the roofs of their homes. Some had chopped holes to get their families onto the roofs."

Then local contractor Herb Jones pulled up to the shore in a motorboat. He called out for someone to help rescue the residents. Jim Crawford stepped forward. "I was rather taken aback that none of the policemen and firemen offered to go with him," Jim said. Thinking his sibling's joke about being a hero was no longer funny, his brother Patrick tried to stop him. "You're crazy," he said. "Do you see the telephone poles floating down the river? You'll never make it."

Ignoring his brother and the obvious dangers, Jim stepped into the boat and grabbed a handheld spotlight. Herb, a skilled boat racer, navigated the swift current. "We started off with the lower porches," Jim said, "bringing back four, five, six people at a time. Then we plucked them from second-storey porches and windows. We tried rescuing the women and children first, but we weren't all that choosy."

They filled up the boat, the sole rescue vehicle, with as many people as possible before heading back to shore. Each time they returned, a fire captain who was also Jim's good friend, asked, "Crawf, are you willing to try it again?"

"I would look over to Herb because we both realized our chances of getting back each time were pretty limited,"

Jim said. "We were bouncing around like corks and we had to avoid stumps and cows and telephones poles coming down the river like toothpicks. 'I'm game if you're game,' I'd say," and they'd set off again.

Patricia Doucette sat with her two young children on the pitched roof of their house bobbing in the water, while her husband Tom tried to help a large elderly lady who lived nearby through the hole he had chopped in the roof. Jim and Herb motored by and helped Patricia and her children into the boat. "We'll come back for you, " Jim yelled to Tom.

But when they returned, the Doucette house had vanished. Using the spotlight, Jim spied the grey-haired neighbour hanging onto a tree branch. "The woman was petrified and she wouldn't let go of the branch," he said. "I was a pretty strong guy: 6 foot 4 inches and 260 pounds, no fat and all muscle. I put my hand underneath her bottom, broke the branch she was holding onto, and pulled her into the boat." Next they rescued Tom, who also huddled in a tree.

Nearby on Fair Glen Crescent, Jean and Bud Irwin, who had celebrated their fifth wedding anniversary the day before, tried to escape after water filled their basement. "We held hands and my husband went just ahead of me," Jean said. "As we stepped onto the driveway, the rush of the water swept him off his feet. I grabbed onto a pipe along the side of the house. He grabbed onto a car handle with his other hand and I pulled him back to the front of the house."

They found the door had slammed shut behind them,

however, and they argued about the cost of replacing the window if Bud broke it. Back in the house, their living room soon filled up with water and they raced up to the second storey. "We were rushing some things upstairs to get them away from the water and I took my roses and set the vase on my husband's dresser because it was higher. I thought if the water came up, it'll still be safe because it was higher than my dresser." Bud had given Jean five roses for their anniversary.

When they got upstairs, Jean devised a plan that would eventually save their lives. She suggested to her husband they knot together a bunch of sheets and attach them to the leg of the bed. Bud warned the sheets would get dirty. "I do the laundry," Jean replied. "Do what I ask, please." Perched on the ledge of the upstairs windowsill, the Irwins waited to be rescued. "I had one arm around the centre post of the window and, in the other, I had an armful of sheets," she said. But still she fretted about her precious roses. "I got to thinking — while we're watching people floating down the river — oh, those roses. I rushed back to the bedroom and moved them from my husband's dresser to my own because my dresser was heavier and his might tip over."

Jean also worried about their next-door neighbour, Charles Ryan, who had waded through the water to save his brand new television set. "Then he couldn't get out," she said. The roof of the Ryan house inclined at a steep slant over the veranda making the front door invisible from the road. "The poor devil, he was hanging from the top of his door and water was lapping at his chin," Jean said. "I kept flashing my light over to him and saying, 'You hang on, Mr. Ryan, everything's going to be fine now. Hang on. We're going to get you help.'"

Every time the boat would come by, Jean would flash the light at the Ryan house to direct Jim and Herb to her neighbour. But the flashlight illuminated the roof over the veranda so Charles was never visible to the two men.

Suddenly the current propelled the Irwin house downstream about 275 metres before it caught on some debris and held. The Ryan house, which the Irwin home had prevented from going downstream, then buckled, sweeping Charles toward Lake Ontario.

At long last, Herb Jones steered his motorboat to rescue the Irwins. However, he and Jim Crawford ran into a problem. "They couldn't get to our window because of the force of the water," Jean said. "So I just yelled, 'Make a good catch, boys' and I threw them the sheets." Fortunately the wind caught the sheets and blew them toward Jim who grabbed onto the end. First Jean, then Bud, climbed down the sheets and into the boat. "Our house was the last one to go down the river," Jean said. "We watched all our neighbours' houses disappear."

With no one left to save, Jim Crawford went back to where he had parked his Pontiac. "It was completely inundated with water," he said. "My mint condition car was a piece of junk."

Shortly after 11 p.m., farther down the river, 26-year-old Etobicoke volunteer firefighter Bryan Mitchell responded to a call outside St. Joseph's Hospital. The dispatcher told him houses had washed out on Scarlett Road and Raymore Drive, an area on the west side of the Humber River, south of Fair Glen Crescent.

Bryan was already exhausted. He had barely recovered from his last rescue at Phillips Road Bridge. He had agreed to "drop by to see what was happening" to someone's car swamped on the approach to the bridge on his way to a flooded dance hall in Thistletown. "This guy was hanging onto a tree for dear life," Bryan said. "I didn't have any equipment in my red fire car. Using a clothesline that people brought out from their houses, I tied it around my waist and swam out 50 feet [15.2 m] in a roaring current. Then the people living in the area pulled us back to safety."

Bryan recognized the man as Jim Eady, a former volunteer fireman. "I put him in my car because he was shivering like a leaf," he said. "His teeth were chattering and he was going into shock." He decided to take Jim Eady to St. Joseph's Hospital. On a good day, the drive down the Queensway to Sunnyside took 15 minutes. "This trip took close to one hour," he said. "There were empty cars in ditches. If you stayed in the middle, you knew you were on the road." He dropped Jim Eady off at the hospital around midnight. When he got back on the two-way radio, the call came in about problems on Raymore Drive so he headed over.

Earlier that evening, some residents on Raymore Drive tried to persuade their neighbours to leave for higher ground.

George Bridger, wading through water often up to his nose, warned people to abandon their homes. A swing bridge over the Humber near Raymore Drive was close to collapse because of the weight of the water. But some people decided instead to listen to a long-time resident who insisted there had never been any previous danger.

Suddenly one end of the bridge snapped away from the abutment, damming the river. The diverted water quickly rose six metres and smashed into the houses on Raymore Drive.

"That's when all hell broke loose," said Bryan, who had arrived on the scene. "Everybody was screaming for help. The bottom end of Raymore Drive near the Humber River had washed out. Instead of going around the bend like a horse-shoe and coming back, it took a shortcut right across the street." A half dozen houses with basements constructed of concrete blocks stood their ground. The rest, built on stilts or pillars like summer cottages, lifted off their foundations and floated down the Humber "like leaves in the rain," Bryan said. He called for help from both the Thistletown and Weston fire stations but all the bridge approaches had already been washed out.

The swollen river kept rising and rising. David Philips, who lived on Raymore Drive, saw houses tumbling into the Humber River with people inside them. "We were forced to stand there and watch people die," he said. "People were sit-ting on the roofs of their houses or on the second floor or in attic windows, screaming 'Help me! Help me!'" Bryan said. "And the winds. You could hardly hear because of the roar of the winds and the roar of the water just rolling down."

Annie and Joe Ward woke up to the sound of water filling their house. They climbed up into the attic with their dog Lassie and sat on the rafters. Joe dug a hole through the roof with a screwdriver and his bare hands. When they squeezed through, the roof began to collapse and the house started floating down the river tangled up with another house. Holding hands, they jumped onto the roof of their neighbours' house.

A helicopter from Ontario Hydro buzzed overhead to rescue people. "Unfortunately, it couldn't do much because of the TV aerials on top of the houses," Bryan said. "When we threw spotlights from the fire truck, the pilots could see they couldn't drop down. But they dangled ropes down for some and we were able to get ropes across to others." Though it took several attempts, a helicopter managed to rescue the Wards from the roof of their neighbours' house.

Bryan and the other firefighters secured ropes to logs and pitched them into the river hoping they would reach the people who were still stranded. Sometimes the firefighters swam out with a rope. One of them single-handedly extended a 10-metre ladder out to a house to rescue some people.

Jack and Molly Anderson had left their house on Raymore Drive while the bridge was still intact but they returned in a motorboat and tried to save the family across the street.

Water engulfed the boat. The Andersons, wearing life jackets, tumbled overboard and were swept downstream.

"For some, there was just nothing we could do." Bryan said. He will never forget the screams of the people he couldn't help as they were swept down the Humber River to Lake Ontario.

South of Raymore Drive on the west side of the Humber, even those rescuing others were not immune from Hazel's ferocity.

Seven volunteer firemen from the Kingsway-Lambton Fire Department had responded to a call on Humber Boulevard, which ran parallel to the river between Dundas and Bloor Streets. As he had missed the pumper truck, fireman Frank Mercer drove himself to the scene where floodwaters had trapped some people in a car.

When he met the crew on the pumper truck, they found no one there. The road ahead appeared flooded so they tried to back up the truck but Frank's car stalled, blocking it. With water rising above the tires and the clutch slipping, the men couldn't manoeuvre the fire truck around the car.

The torrent engulfed the top of the car. Frank Mercer climbed onto the fire truck. Then all of a sudden "a wall of water came from nowhere," slamming the car into the pumper. The firefighters radioed for help.

Police and other firefighters tried unsuccessfully to reach the Kingsway-Lambton firemen with ropes and a boat. When the truck almost overturned, the men shook

The top storey of a severed house lands on a bank of the Humber River after being carried several metres downstream by flood water. Hurricane Hazel caused some of the worst flooding in the province's history.

hands and wished each other good luck. The fierce current carried away the 300-metre fire hose and the truck began to float. Then it tipped over onto its side. The firemen closest to the riverbank grabbed onto some ropes and were pulled ashore. The others jumped into the swiftly moving current and disappeared. Five firefighters perished: Clarence

49

Collins, Frank Mercer, Roy Oliver, David Palmateer, and Angus Small.

Hazel blew out of town the next morning, leaving 81 people dead and 4,000 families homeless. Because of Hurricane Hazel, Toronto experienced its worst flooding in 200 years and Ontario's deadliest natural disaster. On Raymore Drive alone, the hurricane killed 35 people and left 60 families with nowhere to live. The Wards and their dog, Lassie, survived, as did the Andersons because of their life jackets.

On Fair Glen Crescent, Herb Jones and Jim Crawford had saved 50 lives. And when the Irwins went back the next morning to see the damage to their house, Bud found Jean's roses. Not a single drop of water had spilled out of the vase. But the body of their neighbour, Charles Ryan, was found several kilometres down the river.

Chapter 4
Blacked Out:
A Span of 38 Years

The staff at CFTO television were preoccupied with producing the evening newscast when they heard a loud bang. At 5:16 p.m. on November 9, 1965, the studio went black. A technician replacing a part in the complex broadcasting equipment thought he had caused the outage.

The news staff sat in the dark until the generator kicked into operation a few minutes later. Then the teletype machines started spewing out reports of a power outage extending all the way from New York City to Toronto.

The power grid between Canada and the United States had broken down. A surge of electricity flowing from New York into Ontario had suddenly reversed direction, forcing technicians at Toronto's Ontario Hydro to react quickly. They threw the switches to cut off the province's generators from the grid, blacking out most of Southern Ontario. Only the eastern Niagara Peninsula and the area around Windsor, Sarnia, and Chatham kept their power that Tuesday afternoon.

The surge coursed through the rest of the American grid in less than three seconds. It tripped supposedly foolproof circuit breakers and shut down generators in upstate New York, Massachusetts, Vermont, New Hampshire, Connecticut, and New Jersey. The wayward surge disrupted auxiliary power feeds as far west as Montana and as far south as Texas and Florida. The biggest blown fuse in the history of electricity plunged 35 million people in a 207,000-square-kilometre area into darkness.

The initial worry was sabotage. U.S. President Lyndon B. Johnson ordered a massive investigation by the federal power commission of the United States. Called in to probe the black mystery was the Federal Bureau of Investigation as well as the U.S. Defense Department and specialists from both public and private utility systems.

The experts ultimately ruled out sabotage, but they stated that both the U.S. and Canada were vulnerable to enemy attack if — in one blow — power could be knocked out along the eastern seaboard of North America. The power failure "reveals the Achilles heel of the American giant," said the spokesman for the Hague Municipal Power Company. "This could not have happened on any such scale anywhere in Europe, short of earthquake disasters or large floods ..."

In Canada, Prime Minister Lester B. Pearson was preoccupied with another minority government after the election the day before, while Ontario Premier John Robarts strangely issued no statement on the blackout, although during the peak period, the blackout had zapped five million kilowatts or 64 percent of the total capacity of Ontario Hydro — enough power to light 3.5 million homes.

As the two interconnected nations tried to determine the cause of the blackout, the finger pointing began. The Niagara Mohawk Power Co. denied the White House announcement that the blackout was caused by its Niagara Falls, New York, switching plant, while Ontario Hydro's chairman, Ross Strike, accused the U.S. of clamming up.

Whatever the reason for the power blackout, thousands of Torontonians found themselves stranded at the height of rush hour. Despite the immediate activation of the Toronto Transit Commission's emergency subway plan, some commuters were trapped in-between underground tunnels. Others sat on electric streetcars stalled in the middle of intersections. People stuck in elevators in office and apartment buildings waited for rescue. Passengers paced the airport when flights were cancelled. Drivers honked their horns and shook their fists at each other when traffic lights went out. Long line-ups of cars and trucks snaked through the city and traffic slowed to a crawl. Additional police officers were called in to handle the chaos.

The province's electricity company finally restored

power at 6:35 p.m., one hour and 19 minutes after it had gone out. Commuters cheered when transit cars started rolling once again. Ontario Hydro's system supervisor Roy Teal ordered the system rebuilt and cautioned against a power overload. The utility's staff had just heaved a sigh of relief when 19 minutes later, at 6:54 p.m., the power went out again.

Rushing back to police headquarters when the second blackout happened, Police Chief James Mackey appealed to citizens to stay at home as streets were clogged with rush hour traffic. Break and enter detectives were dispatched to bank vaults and jewellery stores to guard the valuable merchandise. Silent burglar alarms had left a fortune in jewellery and cash susceptible to robbers in downtown shops. Despite police efforts, vandals smashed display windows at a furrier and thieves stole cigarettes and watches from a trading company.

The power failure affected everyone. Residents in the Toronto suburbs of North York and Scarborough coped without water as some pumping stations had no backup generators. Food company Christie's tossed out 2,000 half-baked loaves of bread when its ovens stopped working. Three airplanes had to land at an Oshawa airport, east of Toronto, guided by car headlights.

Staff reinforcements started arriving at Ontario Hydro and set to work. They again cut off the province's system to protect it from New York's but maintained contact with

Detroit Edison to keep Western Ontario lit. Nevertheless, the system became unstable again. "It's like twisting an elastic band too much," said Jim Harris, system supervising engineer of Ontario Hydro. At 7:24 p.m., it snapped and Ontario plummeted into darkness for a third time.

The blackout caused teletype machines at Canadian Press, the country's national newswire service, to stop spitting out the news, affecting over 100 newspapers and 275 radio and television stations. Only people wise enough to have batteries on hand could listen to radios to keep informed throughout the darkness and the mayhem. Amateur ham radio operators in Toronto organized a network of communication with Boston, New York, and other U.S. cities.

Things weren't all bad though. In Toronto night court, 50 traffic offenders got a break when the presiding judge dismissed charges against them. Theatre-goers rejoiced when the show went on at the Royal Alexandra Theatre. At movie houses with auxiliary power, film buffs could catch the latest flicks, though some disgruntled patrons still demanded refunds. Honeymooners could stare, dreamy-eyed, at the floodlit Niagara Falls, unaffected by the power blackout.

The engineers at Ontario Hydro Power restored power lines one by one, and some lights returned at 7:12 p.m. in areas of Toronto and elsewhere in the province. About 10 minutes later, the power failed again and remained off in many regions of Ontario, for up to 13 hours.

Ontario wasn't the only place that lost power. About 13

million people in New York and the surrounding area had
no electricity for 10 hours. An estimated 850,000 commuters were stuck below ground in the subway, while another
10,000 waited in Pennsylvania Station. All of the city's 20,000
police officers patrolled the darkened streets, while firefighters with axes and sledgehammers rescued 42 people trapped
in elevators at the Empire State building. Two anti-aircraft
searchlights lit up the Grand Central and Times Square districts but, throughout it all, the Statue of Liberty's gas torch
stayed lit.

The day after the power failures, Ontario Hydro chairman Strike admitted that the utility's decade long association
with the New York and Michigan power systems "may have
developed weaknesses as [they] got bigger." Hydro engineers
studied the breakdown. They determined the distribution
system had to be reorganized before two additional nuclear
generating stations started up, the first one in the fall and the
other six years down the road. Nuclear plants took from 24 to
30 hours to restart. A similar power blackout could be graver
and more prolonged next time, they warned.

Thirty-eight years later, on August 14, 2003, their warning came true. A power swing six times bigger than the one
in 1965 brought Toronto to an abrupt standstill, again during
the evening rush hour.

Michael Chen was sitting in his office near the SkyDome,
waiting for the electricity to come back on. Thinking the outage affected only his office building, he read some reports,

did some filing, and chatted with colleagues to pass the time. He was anxious to get home, however. His 15-year-old son Jonathan was flying back from St. Louis, Missouri, after visiting relatives. It was Jonathan's first trip away from home on his own.

Unbeknownst to Michael and the majority of Torontonians, a power outage had blacked out Southeastern Ontario in nine seconds. Not only was Toronto affected but also Ottawa, New York, Detroit, Cleveland, and most of the Eastern seaboard. Fifty million people had been left without power. And with the second anniversary of the September 11th assault on the World Trade Centre looming, many feared this was another terrorist attack.

Michael and his three colleagues descended the dimly lit stairwell only to vie for space with thousands of other people on the crowded sidewalk in downtown Toronto. The quartet headed east along Front Street West, tossing their jackets over their shoulders. They joined throngs of office workers also heading home. They turned north onto University Avenue. "We tried to get a taxi but it was virtually impossible," Michael said. "The streets were jammed with people. Some were walking. Some were just standing around. Thousands of cars were on the road but they weren't moving."

Rush hour traffic proved to be one of the city's biggest headaches, while the most difficult task was evacuating the subway. Some trains had jolted to a halt in-between stations, others sat in unlit tunnels. At that peak time of the day, around 80 trains operate throughout the city, each with a maximum capacity of 1,500 passengers.

Michael told his buddies, who walked faster than he did, to go ahead. He and his colleague Maggie would walk together. Maggie lived around Finch subway station, the last northbound stop on the Yonge-University-Spadina line that loops north-south in the centre of the city in a U shape. Michael resided in Markham, a suburb northeast of Toronto. However, his car was parked at Finch station. "Our aim was to walk as far as we could until we could catch some kind of transportation."

As they walked along University Avenue, Michael and Maggie saw dozens of commuters turned into ad-hoc traffic cops. All of the city's 1,773 traffic lights had sputtered out as well as all its pedestrian crosswalks. As disgruntled motorists honked in frustration, a Good Samaritan with a whistle in her mouth motioned traffic through an intersection. "People in suits and ties directed traffic," Michael said. "And drivers obeyed them, which was surprising,"

Commuters hung out the windows of the buses try-ing to get some fresh air as the vehicles inched along the street in the rush hour chaos. "We were happy we weren't on those buses," Michael said, "because everybody was really squished and traffic wasn't moving. We just keep walking and walking."

He tried calling his wife Amy several times from his cell phone but he could not get a signal. A massive load of callers hobbled mobile networks at the beginning of the blackout. Other Torontonians with "network busy" messages on their cells lined up 25 deep at phone booths, trying to contact friends and family to get a ride home.

Telephone networks, running on battery and diesel generator backup systems, fared better than cell phone networks during the blackout. Callers trying to leave voice-mail messages, however, became frustrated when they were disconnected or received busy signals.

As the unrelenting sun beat down, their clothes clinging to their bodies and perspiration running down their faces, Michael and Maggie walked with hundreds of others past the hospitals, Queen's Park, and the Royal Ontario Museum. On Avenue Road, clerks handed out bottled water to passers-by at a drug store. Michael and Maggie guzzled down a bottle each, parched and exhausted after walking for two hours. The smell of steamed hot dogs and grilled hamburgers made their stomachs growl but neither wanted to join the long line-up.

They plopped down on the curb to rest from time to time, rubbed their sore feet, and then roused their tired bodies to continue the trek. Reaching Upper Canada College at Avenue Road and Lonsdale Road three hours after they had started out, they found the gates open. Shade trees lined each side of the paths running through the campus, providing Michael and Maggie unexpected and temporary shelter from the hot sun.

Suddenly they spied an unoccupied taxi just after Lawrence Avenue, south of Highway 401. "We thought we were seeing things," Michael said. "We waved madly to get the taxi driver to stop. When he did, we couldn't believe it." By then, they had walked more than 12 kilometres, a distance serviced by 13 subway stations.

As their cabbie darted around the side streets to avoid jammed Yonge Street, they learned that the power failure extended beyond Toronto. At York Mills Road, they got caught in the gridlock. The driver inched the taxi toward Finch and Maggie got out just before it reached the subway station. Then the cabbie dropped Michael off. After paying the driver with a big tip, Michael faced the ordeal of walking again. "That two minutes to my car was very difficult."

He drove his car east through the back streets to get home. None of the traffic lights functioned and cars clogged the streets. "It took me an hour to get home," he said. "A drive that usually takes me 20 minutes."

Meanwhile, Michael's wife, Amy, was in a Scarborough apartment building, picking up her sister for the ride to the airport to pick up Jonathan. When they pushed the button for the elevator, the power suddenly went out. "I thought it was only throughout the building," Amy said. The elevator's backup generator kicked in but they decided to take the stairs. They trudged down 10 flights, hot and irritated, and bumped into the superintendent at the front door. He told them he thought the power outage was restricted to the neighbourhood. "Fortunately I had parked outside and not in the garage," Amy said. "We drove onto the 401 and I turned on the radio. I couldn't get a signal from any of the FM stations."

When Amy switched over to an AM station, she learned that Premier Ernie Eves had declared a province-wide state of emergency and Toronto had activated its Emergency Operations Centre, which had been established in the wake of September 11.

In Chicago, a hot, thirsty, and hungry Jonathon sat on the tarmac waiting for his connecting flight to take off for Toronto. By the time his mother and aunt arrived at the airport, Jonathan had called them. "We're deplaning," he said. "No planes are taking off to Toronto because the airport is shut down." With no power to run metal detectors and X-ray machines, airports in 12 major cities in Canada and the United States had shut down or partially closed.

Customer service staff at Toronto's Pearson International Airport contended with line-ups of irate passengers upset about both the power outage and the total breakdown of Air Canada's computerized control centre. Amy worried she might be stuck at the airport for hours, so decided to return home. After dropping off her sister, she continued her trek, arriving in Markham after Michael. She drove into the driveway and then just sat there.

The exhausted Chens ate sandwiches for dinner, then fell asleep in the cool of the basement. The hum of the air conditioner woke Michael up around 5:30 a.m. Flights into

Pearson International Airport had resumed, so Michael and Amy left for the airport to pick Jonathan up. The traffic lights in Markham still weren't functioning. Cars and trucks had to stop at each intersection and proceed cautiously. "Once we got on the highway, however, we had no trouble getting out to the airport," Amy said. "But finding Jonathan was another story."

When he finally arrived in Toronto after spending the night in the Chicago airport, Jonathan had been so tired he had fallen asleep on one of the couches. Amy said, "It took us almost an hour to find him." Then the Chens went to buy boxes and boxes of candles to be prepared for the next blackout.

When the power failed, Jill Stevens was chatting on the telephone in her office on the 14th floor of the Royal Bank Plaza at Bay and Wellington Streets in downtown Toronto. Off on vacation the next day, she had lots of calls to make and some projects to finish before she left. She waited with her colleagues, hoping the power would be restored, since many of them needed public transportation to get back home. No one relished the idea of walking to somewhere like Oakville, a bedroom community 40 kilometres west of Toronto.

Fortunately, around 7 p.m., a colleague offered to give Jill a ride home to Eglinton and Bathurst. "It was a madhouse down on Bay Street," Jill said. "There were people everywhere. It was pretty slow going because all the lights were out and cars were everywhere." Jill arrived at her apartment building to find only one elevator worked, and a lot of people waiting for it. She tackled the stairs, stopping often to catch her breath, as she made her way to the 15th floor. "It was so hot," she said.

Jill drove back downtown later that evening to shut down her computer. Although power had been restored to some parts of the city, the signal lights were still out where she lived. As Jill got closer to downtown, more and more of them were working. "On Dufferin Street, there was a huge line-up at this beer store," she said. "I couldn't believe that the first thing people did when the power came back on was go to a beer store."

Downtown, on the other hand, was like a ghost town. "There was nobody around," she said. "It was barren and eerie." But when Jill drove up Yonge Street to get home again and pack for her holiday, all the billboards and office buildings were lit up. She commented: "Most of Toronto didn't have power and here's where our power was going."

In the meantime, in the Toronto suburb of North York, Kathy Okawara was making the best of things during the blackout. She dug up the propane stove she and her husband Harvey used for camping, brewed up some coffee, and invited the neighbours over. "They were grateful," Kathy said. The Okawaras then barbecued some meat from the defrosting refrigerator, before falling asleep in the dark. They woke up to a humming fridge and blasts of cold air from the air conditioner.

That morning, on the second day of the blackout, Kathy and Harvey set out in their car for St. Marys, Ontario. They had tickets for the Stratford Festival and planned to stay in a bed and breakfast in nearby St. Marys to enjoy the town's architecture. Though partial blackouts still existed in some areas of the province, the lights had come back on in St. Marys. Kathy said, "We were out shopping in the afternoon. The townspeople went from store to store asking the owners to shut off any lights they didn't really need. As a result, the stores were pretty dark and the doors to all the shops were open. I was impressed that in this small town they were all obeying without question."

Premier Ernie Eves had asked *all* Ontarians to conserve electricity for the next couple of days. The older nuclear-generating plants would be delayed in restarting — a concern expressed in 1965 — and full power could not be provided until the following week. A spokesperson for the New York Independent System Operator, which managed the state's grid, said: "The blackout of 1965 was triggered by an 800-megawatt power swing. What we're looking at (now) from the preliminary data ... is a power swing of about 5,000 megawatts out of Ontario." The second power swing, 38 years later, had indeed been much more powerful and prolonged than the first one — just as experts had warned.

When Trudy Olsen dropped her son off for work at a Burlington video store, it was dark. The lights were also off in the convenience store next door. And yet, "a group of women was loading up their car with ice and bottles of water and batteries," Trudy said. When she overheard them saying the power had gone out all over the place and terrorists might be responsible, she became alarmed. She even started to panic when she realized she couldn't buy anything because all the automatic bank machines would be down. Fortunately Trudy had some cash so she also loaded up with ice and water and batteries and headed off to her local grocery store. "The doors were locked," she said. "They thought something evil had happened."

When she got home, Trudy called her cousin Alison in Montreal for expert advice. Alison had been through the ice storm in 1998, which had left areas of the province of Quebec without electricity from a few days to a couple of months. Fortunately, it wasn't winter in Toronto but her cousin advised her to make sure she had a full tank of propane for the barbecue. Trudy jumped in the car and drove from gas station to gas station trying to find one that sold propane.

Trudy's husband, Jenn, a volunteer policeman, arrived home to learn he had to report for duty at his police auxiliary. The mayor of Burlington, the chief of police, council members, and the fire chief were troubleshooting about the blackout at the Halton Regional Headquarters in Oakville, part of the Greater Toronto Area. With propane tanks providing auxiliary power, the television at headquarters had been turned to CNN. "That was the first time I saw how the power blackout was affecting the city," he said.

Later that night, after Trudy learned that some areas east of Burlington had power, she set off to get some gas. "It was kind of scary driving there because there were no streetlights. I found a huge line-up at the pumps." When Jenn finished his volunteer stint at about 1 a.m. and drove home, he experienced something similar. "It was the eeriest feeling that I've ever had," he said. "Driving in absolute pitch black. Not a house light on. Not a street light on. And I was the only car out there."

But that wasn't the worst of it, he knew. "If we had had to go on another two days, we would have run out of food, run out of money, run out of water. Panic would have set in. Without power and electricity, we're in big trouble. To this day, we keep water and batteries and flashlights and candles in the house," he said. "I hope it's something we don't have to go through again."

Unplugged by the largest blackout in North American history, the major metropolis of Toronto was thrown into chaos and brought almost to a standstill. Without warning, an electricity system managed by two of the world's super-powers had failed not once but twice in 38 years. In 2003, the security of more than 50 million people had been affected —15 million more than in 1965. In a power-hungry province like Ontario, the question became: when would the next disaster occur?

Chapter 5
Air Canada Crash

Captain Peter Hamilton prepared to land the aircraft at Toronto's Malton Airport on July 5, 1970. The 50-minute early morning flight from Montreal with 100 passengers and nine crew on board had been routine. After picking up 125 more passengers in Toronto, the plane would be close to capacity and would continue on to Los Angeles.

Peter piloted the stretch DC-8 to an altitude of 8,000 metres over Ottawa, cruising at 850 kilometres per hour. Beginning the slow descent to Toronto over Peterborough, he reduced the power by half, descended to an altitude of 5,000 metres, and turned south. The 49-year-old pilot handled the spanking new, four-engine aircraft with ease.

During World War II, he had been a bomber pilot, and he had already racked up 3,000 flying hours on DC-8s after joining Air Canada (AC) in 1946.

In the cockpit with him were two other pilots. First Officer Donald Rowland, 39 years old, was also very experienced, with over 5,500 hours on DC-8 aircraft that had been in service over 10 years. Second Officer H. Gordon Hill had flown more than 1,000 hours.

Peter and Donald had worked together on previous flights but they had butted heads over one issue: when to deploy the ground spoiler panels on the wings of the DC-8. When deployed, these panels disrupted the air flowing over the wings and helped the aircraft to settle onto the runway after landing.

The Air Canada operating manual at the time only instructed crew to arm (or activate) the spoiler panels when the aircraft was 1,000 feet (304.8 metres) or more above the ground. Concerned that premature deployment could cause the aircraft to "drop like a dead bird," both pilots chose to ignore this company directive. But, in the days before trusted automated systems, one preferred to extend the spoiler panels on the ground just *after* touching down for a smoother landing. The other liked to arm them on the flare, that is, just *before* touching the ground. To complicate matters, the same lever was *lifted* to arm, and *pulled* to deploy, the spoiler panels.

With the three pilots on board AC Flight 621 were six

flight attendants, all based in Montreal. They planned to work the daily return flight from Los Angeles, known as the "California Galaxy," layover in Toronto for the night, then work the flight back to Montreal the following day.

Despite the DC-8 being the largest airliner available until the 747 eclipsed it the following year, the California Galaxy was packed that day. Air travel had boomed in the previous decade and didn't show any signs of stopping. The passengers boarding in Montreal were mostly holidaying Quebecers or Californians returning home from Canada.

The only passenger in first class, Gilles Labonté, made frequent trips to Los Angeles. As president of Allergan Canada, Ltd., a pharmaceutical company, he was flying to the American head office for meetings.

On board were 21 children, many of them flying for the first time. One 11-year-old, Lynn Boosamra, was travelling on her own to visit her sister in Los Angeles. It was her first flight.

Gilles Raymond was travelling by himself. The 16-year-old had been the last person to board the aircraft before the doors shut. His parents, who had driven him to the airport from Boucherville, had walked him to the gate to ensure he secured a seat. Gilles had worked after school all winter to save money to visit his aunt in Los Angeles. When he had discovered he was $60 short for the youth standby ticket, his mother lent him the money in exchange for babysitting his brother and two younger sisters when he returned.

Susie Wong was on her first airplane ride, too, thanks

to her doting grandparents. They were going to spend the summer in San Francisco at the home of grandmother Ngar-Quon Wong's sister. Mr. and Mrs. Wong had convinced the 11-year-old's parents to let their granddaughter accompany them — they said they would miss the family too much if they went alone.

Celia Sultan rocked her four-month-old baby, Gerald. She was also travelling with her two-year-old son Robert. They were returning home to Los Angeles after visiting Celia's parents.

Bernard Gee was on the first leg of an extended trip to Asia. After seeing Expo '70 in Osaka, he planned to visit other Asian countries. Sister Madeleine Grenier, a teacher at Montreal's Mont Jésus-Marie d'Outremont, was not on vacation but travelling to Los Angeles to see her 72-year-old mother who was ill.

In good company with the many honeymooners on board was flight attendant Gundi Wieczorek. She was a newlywed herself — again. She and her husband, Eric, had first married in Puerto Rico but since the ceremony hadn't been recognized in Canada, they had tied the knot again the month before. That morning they had driven to the airport together. Eric had hugged and kissed Gundi goodbye before starting his own shift as a passenger agent for Canadian Pacific Airlines.

Two honeymooning couples, the Adams and the Mailhiots, had been married the day before. Gustav and

Karoline Maitz were also on a honeymoon trip — 20 years after getting married — to see Karoline's daughter and grandchild in Los Angeles.

Two other happy couples on board were friends: the Leclaires and the Roberts. When the Roberts had unexpectedly arrived from Los Angeles, Oscar and Marie Rose Leclaire had cancelled their previous booking to Los Angeles for July 2. The high school teachers had extended their hospitality and given a tour of Montreal to their American friends, who had then convinced them to fly with them to Los Angeles. Now the foursome was on their way to California.

Another pair, Lewella and Linda Earle, were not going to California but to Cleveland, where they both had boyfriends. In Toronto, they were planning to make the transfer for the final leg of their trip. The twin sisters did everything together. They were both medical secretaries at Montreal's Royal Victoria Hospital and they also attended Sir George Williams University at night.

Dr. Gabriel Desmarais and his wife Brigitte were flying to Los Angeles to find an apartment. The chief gynaecologist at Charles Lemoyne Hospital on Montreal's south shore was planning to further his studies in California.

Passenger Mark Simon was supposed to be part of a couple travelling that day but he had convinced his wife Penny to cancel her reservation home. Instead she was going to extend her visit with his parents to attend a family wedding in Montreal, and spend more time with their 10-year-old son

Mark, Jr., before he attended a Montreal summer camp.

Former Montrealer Jeannine Chapdelaine was travelling without her husband Betrand because he had found a new job as a gas station attendant in Los Angeles. They had moved there nearly a year ago, but two months before their coffee shop had burned to the ground. Jeannine had gone back to Montreal where they kept a safety deposit box to cash in some bonds — their life savings. Now she was returning home with their two young children, Joanne and Mario, after visiting her parents for two weeks in Drummondville, south of Montreal. Inside the cosmetic case stowed under the seat in front of her was $25,000 in cash.

Some Air Canada employees, travelling on passes, were also on board. Reginald Whittingham, a storeman at the airline, was on his way to Disneyland with his wife, Jeannie, and 12-year-old son, John. Leonard Benson, an equipment manager, was going to Los Angeles on business, accompanied by his wife and two children, Helen, 12, and Ricky, 9. Dallas Woodward, manager of flight simulators, was also combining business with pleasure on his Los Angeles trip. His mother lived in Los Angeles.

Mechanic Gilles Decarie and his wife Alice were on airline passes to California for a two-week vacation with their three children. Gilles sat with fellow mechanic Roland Bélanger who was also taking his wife Hélène and their family to Disneyland. Behind them sat their wives and two rows down, 11-year-old Linda Decarie sat with

Roseanne Bélanger, 10. A friend was looking after Linda's pet rabbit while Pompom, the family dog, was staying with neighbours.

Across the aisle, the teenaged sons of the Decaries, Luke and Mark, sat together as did the Bélanger sons, Jacques and Jean. For some reason, the Belanger boys had written a will before leaving on vacation, leaving their sports equipment, typewriter, tape recorder, and other possessions to their cousins and friends.

Lead station attendant Gaetan Beaudin had tried to get on the California flight the day before but it had been fully booked. Even though he had just returned from a European vacation, he was extending his holidays to visit his aunt and uncle, leaving his wife Ninon at home with their two-and-a-half-year-old boy, Stephen.

Up front in the cockpit, preparing for landing, Captain Hamilton switched on the red seat belt light. The attendants walked down the aisle ensuring tray tables were tucked away and seatbelts were fastened. Then they strapped themselves into their seats.

About 13 kilometres from the Toronto airport, Captain Hamilton dropped the landing gear. First Officer Rowland stretched in his seat. "Nice day," he said. It was a brilliant, sunny day with a temperature of 22 degrees Celsius. "Beautiful," Captain Hamilton replied.

As they made their final approach, the aircraft cruised at 400 kilometres per hour, 1,800 metres above Toronto.

Rowland pointed out the city's High Park area — a splash of green among paved roads and concrete high-rises — and sparkling blue Lake Ontario. Second Officer Hill mentioned how expensive Toronto's houses were compared to those of Montreal. Only a month ago, he had transferred to Montreal from Toronto. He stopped mid-sentence when the air traffic controller's voice came over the radio. AC 621 was cleared to land on the airport's longest runway, number 32.

It was time for Air Canada's pre-landing checklist. Second Officer Hill said, "Spoilers to go and the boards clear."

Captain Hamilton responded, "Okay. Brakes three green, four pressures, spoilers on the flare."

First Officer Rowland said, "No, on the ground."

Peter said, "Give them to me on the flare. I have given up. I am tired of fighting it."

First Officer Rowland laughed. Prior to dropping the landing gear, they'd had another brief debate about what spoiler technique to use.

Captain Hamilton reduced speed and at 8:02 a.m., gave the okay to arm the spoilers. Eighteen metres over the runway, the first officer reached for the spoiler control lever. But instead of lifting the lever on the two-way handle — to arm the spoiler panels — Donald pulled it and opened them in the air.

Captain Hamilton yelled, "No! No! No!"

"Sorry, oh sorry, Pete!" said the first officer, instantly

realizing his mistake. Premature deployment of the spoilers before landing caused the aircraft to drop rapidly — exactly what they had both feared. It struck the runway with a jolt, the right wing hitting the ground.

As the jolted passengers screamed and the children wailed in fright, Hamilton had to make a split-second decision: abort the landing or bring the big jet to a stop without overshooting the runway. Unfortunately, due to the DC-8's design, he couldn't see the engines or the wings from the cockpit. He didn't know that one of his four engines had fallen off and the escaping fuel had ignited.

From the Toronto terminal, the 125 passengers waiting at Gate 27 to join the California Galaxy had a clear view of Runway 32. So did the Air Canada gate agents and the ground crews on the tarmac. Everyone fell silent except for a few gasps.

Captain Hamilton had decided to abort the landing, and immediately applied full power to all the remaining engines, raising the nose of the aircraft. He told the controller he wanted to attempt another landing on Runway 32. "We'll go around. I think we're all right," he said. He ordered the landing gear up and headed northwest. The jet climbed to 945 metres, trailing smoke and fire.

The air traffic controller stated calmly, "The runway is closed. Debris on the runway." He gave the captain instructions to Runway 23 instead.

Captain Hamilton still didn't know one of the engines

was the runway debris but he realized he had no power to Number 4. When Second Officer Hill told him the fuel flow meter was low, he ordered it shut down.

As the plane veered northeast, an explosion occurred in the right wing and sheets of metal tumbled to the earth. First Officer Rowland repeated, "Pete, sorry."

"All right," the captain answered simply, far too busy wrestling with a crippled aircraft and weighing his options. Flying without one or even two engines was not out of the question.

Underneath the flight path, Wilbur and Bea Duncan were standing on the front lawn of their bungalow, having just gotten out of bed. "Look out," Mrs. Duncan screamed. A three-metre section of the wing crashed through their roof and into the bedroom, scattering debris throughout the house.

Six seconds later, a second explosion occurred on the plane. It had been two-and-a-half minutes since the initial touchdown. Engine No. 3 plummeted to the ground in flames.

From the putting green of the Woodbridge Golf and Country Club, W. H. Briggs looked up when he heard a noise and saw the engine drop. "It seemed to follow the plane even though it was detached and on fire," he said. "I wanted to get sick."

When the air traffic controller asked, "The status of your aircraft, please," the captain could only reply, "We've got an explosion."

"Oh, God," First Officer Rowland said, as 11 kilometres from the airport, a third explosion ripped off most of the right wing and the crew's hopes.

Below the crippled airplane was the Burgsma farm. John Burgsma was listening to the radio when he heard a loud boom. He ran to the window. "I saw this fiery red, comet like thing coming over the pine trees from the west ... It was coming real fast. One wing was in flames. I couldn't see the other." He screamed to his parents and seven brothers and sisters who were still sleeping, "Get out of the house!"

Another unwitting spectator, Michael Matyas, was driving his son to the airport along Highway 7. "Then the plane just nose-dived right down," he said. "Big, black smoke came up when it hit the ground."

The DC-8 missed the Burgsma farmhouse by less than 50 metres. The aircraft exploded when it struck their barley and alfalfa fields at over 400 kilometres per hour. The crash spewed passengers and airplane parts for almost a third of a kilometre and dug a three-metre crater. Sytze Burgsma, John's father, went to investigate. "There was a huge, black billow of cloud like a shroud over the whole area, but there were no screams."

The crash killed all passengers and crew on board Air Canada Flight 621. Nearly all the bodies were scorched beyond recognition. The badly mangled bodies of 21 of the passengers could not be identified at all; they were buried in a common grave in Toronto's Mount Pleasant Cemetery.

The crash of AC 621 was the Toronto airport's deadliest disaster and one of Canada's worst aviation accidents.

The subsequent inquiry into AC 621's crash, however, found a serious design flaw in the DC-8 ground spoilers: the same lever was used for two functions. McDonnell Douglas, the manufacturer of the aircraft, and Air Canada were cited for negligence in their failure to warn in the operating manuals of the hazard of extending the ground spoilers when the aircraft was in flight and close to the ground. Other contributing circumstances were the Ministry of Transport's acceptance and approval of the design of the ground spoiler system and its failure to detect the deficiencies in both the manufacturer's and Air Canada's flight manuals.

After the crash, warning stickers were placed in DC-8 cockpits to prevent ground spoilers from being operated while a plane was in flight. Nevertheless, three years later, it happened again when another first officer inadvertently deployed the ground spoilers of an Icelandic Airlines DC-8. The aircraft was positioned 12 metres above the runway of New York's John F. Kennedy International Airport. The airplane fell rapidly and struck the ground tail first. No one died, but a number of passengers suffered serious injuries.

The U.S. National Transportation Safety Board determined that the decision of the captain to arm the spoilers just before landing was a contributing factor. The departure from normal procedures like what occurred on AC 621 forced the crew to respond quickly with insufficient time for corrective action. As a result of the accident, all DC-8s were equipped with locking collars to prevent in-flight deployment of spoilers. But it was too late for the 109 Toronto-bound passengers and crew of the California Galaxy on July 5, 1970.

Chapter 6
Subway Catastrophe

On August 11, 1995, at the Downsview subway station, newlywed Hui Xian Lin gripped her husband Van's hand as rush hour commuters brushed past them. Sandy, as she was nicknamed, had joined Van from Vietnam a year before, after an eight-month courtship by correspondence. They managed to get a seat together on the last car of Run 34 and snuggled close.

They were heading to Chinatown for dinner at their favourite restaurant, as they did every Friday after cashing their cheques from the North York upholstery factory that employed them both. Sandy had something new to celebrate that night. Her supervisor had agreed to let her work more hours. She was looking forward to mailing some extra money from her seamstress job to her mother back home.

Subway Catastrophe

Before the subway doors closed, Kinga Szabo clambered on board and slumped into a seat. She had been complaining to relatives about being tired from household responsibilities and the long hours at the bank where she worked. It wasn't as if she was unaccustomed to hard work. On the Romanian women's basketball team, she had trained many hours for the 1976 Montreal Olympics. Afterward, she had defected to Canada. But now 43, she needed a break and would finally get it this weekend. She and her husband Paul planned to leave with their six-year-old son Peter for the Muskokas the next morning.

Two stops south, at Yorkdale station on the Yonge-University-Spadina line, Lemuel Layda boarded the same last car of the six-car train. He manoeuvred his way to the rear. After waiting tables all day at a shopping mall restaurant, he grabbed an available seat to get off his feet for a while.

Roberto Reyes and his wife Christina Munar Reyes followed Lemuel into the car. Loaded down with shopping bags, the couple in their thirties sat across from Lemuel and continued a lively conversation. Lemuel recognized the language as Tagalog, his native tongue from the Philippines, but he only listened to them for a short time before he dozed off.

Christina appreciated any time she could spend with Roberto before going to work to support the rest of her family in the Philippines. The vivacious brunette worked as a health care worker for seniors during the week and at a drug store on the weekends. The couple had married four years before in the Philippines, but Roberto had arrived in Canada only three months ago. Though he had been a construction supervisor back home, he could only get a job cleaning a restaurant here. He was still trying to adjust to life in the city where Christina had lived for seven years.

Farther down the line, at St. Clair Avenue West station, Jean McNab followed her five-year-old son, Ricky Roche, into the last car. Ricky clambered into a seat in the front of the tram and Jean sat down beside him. Another passenger, Estevan Fiugoni, couldn't help but smile at the energetic little boy as he took a seat at the rear of the car. The 45-year-old was heading downtown to his janitor's job.

Southbound for the next stop at Dupont, operator Domenic DeSantis drove Run 34 through one of the longest underground stretches of the subway system. He guided it uphill into the tunnel, took a sharp left, and then swung right around a blind corner before straightening the train out. Located hundreds of metres below ground, this graded and curved section is also one of the deepest in the Toronto transit system. Just ahead, the signal light beamed red. DeSantis stepped on the brakes to bring the tram to a halt.

Not far behind, Robert Jeffery operated Run 35 with another six cars. He clenched the steering wheel tightly. It was his second day on the job for which he had received 12 days of training. For 15 months, he had driven Toronto Transit buses, a subway driver pre-requisite, with a clean record. Yesterday, however, he had run through a double red signal light and a route supervisor had reviewed operating procedures with him. A report had not been filed as the rookie had been told the light was a "known signal problem," so he had not been disciplined for the violation.

Leaving Wilson station, Jeffery looked at his watch and realized he was four minutes behind schedule. If the train fell behind, he could be reprimanded. He guided the train into St. Clair Avenue West station. After picking up some passengers, he proceeded to Dupont station at 56 kilometres per hour, 8 kilometres over the speed limit. He barrelled down the track through three sets of red lights, and flew around the blind curve into the descent to Dupont. Each time Jeffery went through a red light, the trip arms that should have triggered emergency brakes to avoid collisions failed to activate. Suddenly Jeffery saw Run 34 dead ahead. Slamming on the brakes, he kept pumping the pedal in a desperate attempt to stop his tram. It struck the rear of Run 34 at 6:02 p.m.

The impact shoved the stationary train, Run 34, 10 metres down the track. Run 35 split into a V and its floor slid underneath the immobile train. The two trains fused together and spiked upward toward the ceiling of the tunnel. The interconnected trams plugged the entire tunnel, sealing off the airflow. "We both went flying," said Mike Borselaw, a Toronto high school student, who had boarded at Yorkville with his girlfriend.

The lights on the trains went out and hundreds of terrified passengers screamed into the darkness. Estevan Fiugoni, who had boarded the train with Jean McNab and her son Ricky said, "I could hear the little boy screaming." After about three minutes, there was silence, he said. Then two electrical cables exploded. "We could see the light, hear the bang, and smell the smoke," Estevan said. "We thought the explosion was a bomb."

The collision pitched Lemuel Layda, sitting in the last car of the front train, to the middle of the floor. "The car just formed a cave when it was smashed." Then he heard screams for help in his native language. "Help me! Help us! God help us!" Roberto Reyes yelled in Tagalog. Two metal pieces were pinning his torso. In the wreckage nearby, Lemuel could see only the arms of Roberto's wife Christina poking through. Lemuel tried to talk to her but she didn't answer. "I was squeezing her hand. She was still hot." Lemuel then tried to remove Roberto from the debris, telling him to keep calm. Roberto could only moan in pain, crying that his wife was dead.

One of a crew of three, fireman Ken Bodrug rushed down three flights of stairs to the subway platform underground, lugging oxygen ventilators and a first-aid kit.

The acting captain of Toronto fire station Pumper 23 had received a call on the way back from a blaze to attend to a couple of people collapsed at Dupont station. The crew checked both northbound and southbound platforms but saw no one collapsed. They trudged back upstairs. The ticket taker urged them to go to the far end of the southbound platform.

Following his instructions, they met a Toronto Transit

supervisor talking on the phone and two maintenance workers. When he saw the firefighters, the supervisor looked surprised. As far as he was aware, there wasn't any problem. The three firemen shuffled farther up the stifling subway tunnel, weighed down by air packs, masks, rubber boots, and liners in their coats. Sweat poured down their faces. Their flashlights glowed eerily in the cavern, pitch black from the shut off of the power.

Ken smelled burnt wires and then an overwhelming stench of vomit. He also noticed wisps of grey smoke. Sensing disaster, he ran to an emergency phone in the tunnel and called for more help. As he put down the receiver, he saw passengers stumbling like zombies down the track.

Shortly after 6 p.m. at Metro ambulance services, the light flickered on dispatcher Christine Gathercoe's telephone console. The caller, a Toronto Transit Commission (TTC) transit control operator responsible for contacting emergency response agencies, reported "fumes on the train" in the subway and requested an ambulance. Christine told fellow dispatchers Bunny Tetzlaff and Rob Gathercoe, her husband, about the call. Without knowing exactly what the problem could be, she dispatched a team of paramedics to Dupont station.

The TTC hadn't experienced many incidents over its history. In 1976, the subway closed down for two days after an arsonist set Christie station on fire. In two separate incidents in January 1987, a train derailed and a water pipe burst.

Smoke from overheated train brakes filled a tunnel in March 1992 and a fire occurred at Sheppard station in July 1995.

More calls for help started to flood into ambulance services, but the callers confused the dispatchers. Each caller mentioned a different location in the subway system: St. Clair, Russell Hill, Sir Winston Churchill Park. The dispatchers later learned that Russell Hill was an emergency exit from St. Clair Avenue West station. Another emergency exit led to the west side of Sir Winston Churchill Park at the southeast corner of St. Clair Avenue West and Spadina Road.

About 20 minutes after the first call came in, Bunny Tetzlaff took another call from communications at the Toronto Transit Commission. She then had to inform her supervisor that two, or possibly three, subway trains had collided in a tunnel.

At around the same time, Toronto police Sergeant Ed Lamch was taking a breather after responding to a major fire on Queen Street. He glanced at the computer screen in his patrol car. The message scrolling across indicated police were needed for crowd control at St. George, the first subway station south of Dupont. Toronto Transit Commission workers were concerned about an accident, since no trains had appeared for a while and scores of commuters had jammed the station. The officer decided to investigate at the station north of St. George — Dupont — rather than deal with irritated passengers.

At Dupont, he walked cautiously downstairs. After 24

years of experience, he sensed something was wrong, and sure enough, he met a visibly upset policeman emerging from the tunnel. His colleague pointed north. There had been an accident. People were hurt and the officer thought some were dead.

The narrow tunnel, dimly lit by flickering emergency lighting, sloped uphill. Unsure whether the power had been turned off, Sergeant Lamch edged his way along a small ledge on the side of the tunnel to avoid the high voltage track. He could barely breath in the moist hot air. A sparse blue mist hung around his midsection. He crept along for several kilometres and then he spied a train ahead with blaring headlights. "It was a ghost train in the dark," he said.

He climbed on board and walked through the empty cars of the first train until he reached the crash scene. He heard people crying and, every once in a while, steel groaning. He saw a man pinned under the ruins with a dead woman beside him. Blood smeared the floor of the car. To reach the next car, he had to crawl on his belly underneath the train where he found more people trapped. Sergeant Lamch would remain on the scene for the next 14 hours.

The first of the paramedics to arrive in the tunnel spotted a Toronto Transit Commission worker at the end of the platform. There had been a crash, he told them, and more paramedics were urgently needed. Unable to use their cell phones underground, one of the paramedics dashed upstairs to call ambulance services from a public phone.

Paramedic Patti Whitten and her partner, Craig Wilson, were near the Don Valley Parkway and the 401, and halfway through a 12-hour shift when they got the call. They had started at 11 a.m. that Friday morning. As the temperature had hit 30 degrees Celsius, Patti was looking forward to the sun setting to cool off the muggy city. She turned on the siren and followed the directions to Nordheimer Ravine, situated in Sir Winston Churchill Park, north of Casa Loma near the Spadina Road Bridge. She had never been there before.

At the ravine, they found a massive contingent of fire trucks, police cars, and ambulances already there. They saw 50 or 60 dazed passengers emerging from the emergency exit, struggling up the hill. Some were streaked with blood. Soot covered their faces, their hair, and their clothes like coal miners. Arms wrapped around waists, the uninjured were helping the injured.

Patti and Craig headed into the subway hauling a 45-kilogram bag of life support equipment. Down and down they went into one of the deepest tunnels in the TTC system. "It was pitch dark down there and a bit smoky," Patti said. The faint lighting forced them to proceed cautiously. When they reached the floor of the humid, dirty tunnel, someone yelled, "Over here." They walked toward the sound, hiking uphill the length of about eight subway cars.

They found a gargantuan tangle of steel and twisted metal. The scene was later described as "two aluminum pop cans being crushed together" by Acting Fire Chief Peter

Ferguson. Patti and Craig squeezed through the openings between the tunnel and the fused trains, then crawled under the cars to reach the victims. About a dozen people had arrived ahead of them: firefighters, police officers, TTC security, and two other crews of paramedics.

One paramedic attended to five-year-old Ricky Roche. Pinned under a seat, the boy cried in pain. Beside him, his mother, Jean McNab, moaned. She had a pole speared through her leg. Another paramedic tried to reassure her. Nearby, former elite basketball player, Kinga Szabo, lay crushed to death. Patti and Craig tried to cover her body in the confined area. "It was like working in a sardine can," said Patti, a newly trained level three paramedic. Until doctors arrived, she was the highest trained medical person at the crash site.

Like two steel mattresses, the wreckage entombed strangers Roberto Reyes and Sandy Lin from the waist down. Sandy hung upside down, dangling from her hips. Trying to make the woman as comfortable as possible, "we fashioned a KED," Patti said. "It's an extraction device like a jacket that's placed on the upper body to hold the neck in position. After that was on her, Craig and I took turns, standing on either side of her, holding her up so she could lay flat." However, they couldn't see Sandy's legs, so they crawled under the train and beamed flashlights up trying to find any bleeding. "None was visible," said Patti.

"To get to Roberto, we had to crawl under one train and

up the other side," Patti said. "We had to move carefully with all the sharp exposed metal. He was tangled in the wreckage, lying on his stomach. We got some pillows and put them under his upper body." But unlike what they had been able to do with Sandy, the paramedics couldn't get to his lower body to see his injuries. "Fortunately his legs weren't bleeding, though it was a bit of a puzzle," Patti said.

Roberto's wife, Christina Reyes, had died instantly and lay wedged in the ruins. "Her arm was exposed and that was all," Patti said.

The firefighters toiled furiously to free the trapped victims. Some used power tools, such as the Jaws of Life, to cut away the tons of sharp, twisted metal that jutted helter skelter from the wreckage. Others wielded chains, winches, pulleys, and battering rams. The constant drilling and the steady crunch of steel drowned out every other sound.

Subway workers had immediately shut off the power when the accident occurred, cutting off ventilation fans. The collision had also sealed off air ducts. The rescue crews had to cope with a build up of stifling stale air and intense heat. "Once the emergency lighting got set up, it must have been 130 [54 °C] or 140 [60 °C] degrees down there," Patti said. "I was soaked from the outside in. You'd put your hand up over your head to reach for something and sweat would pour out of your glove." Because of the sauna-like conditions, many rescuers could only tolerate working underground for 10 minutes at a time.

Within an hour, firefighters had extracted Jean McNab and her son and they were carried away on stretchers. Waiting for Roberto and Sandy to be freed was stressful and seemed endless for the paramedics. "Fire[fighters] are so good about getting people out of car wrecks," Patti said. "Generally they do it within half an hour. But the time kept going on and on because the metal was so difficult to get at and cut. Fire kept telling us, 'It'll be another half hour.'"

Only a dozen people, working side by side and hunched over, could fit into the cleared area around each victim. The rescue workers also encountered countless complications that required many precautions. They had to ensure that any removal of a piece of debris from around Sandy or Roberto would not harm the other trapped person. "Whenever a section was removed, it was passed out from hand to hand by whoever was the closest — a paramedic or a firefighter," Patti said.

"If we needed more equipment," she said, "an assembly line of paramedics would run down the tunnel and up to the top, get it, and bring it back down to us." Several rescuers delivered tools to the crash site by lying on their backs and passing the equipment in a human chain under the subway cars.

Patti and Craig continued to monitor Sandy and Roberto's vital signs, administer morphine for their pain, talk to them, and reassure them. "They were both conscious and alert," Patti said. "They weren't screaming. However, we couldn't give them a lot of water in the event they'd vomit.

We would wet their lips with these electrical instrument swabs we had." Every 15 minutes, their vital signs had to be monitored to determine how much morphine could be given to them. "With all the noise, it was impossible to hear a blood pressure," Patti said. "We'd ask the firemen to stop so we could listen to it. On the mark, everyone would stop. Then away they would go again."

Unauthorized to perform blood transfusions, the paramedics sent for more help. Drs. Andrew McCallum and Doug Chisholm arrived at about 11 p.m. The two doctors from Sunnybrook Hospital crawled on their stomachs underneath the mangled debris to reach the two trapped victims. Dr. McCallum couldn't give a transfusion immediately to Sandy, though she needed it the most. The wreckage impeded his access to her. Eventually he decided one of her legs had to be amputated to free her from the steel. Rescue workers held a klieg light over her and he performed the amputation with an electric saw. Sergeant Lamch, who had stayed on duty, said, "It sounded like a Skil saw. Like you hear on a construction site."

Despite the efforts to save her, Sandy died shortly after being transported above ground. Patti and Craig remained with her until she died. "She bled somewhere in her leg but we couldn't find the bleeding," Patti said. "Eventually people just can't compensate anymore and they die. We just didn't know. It was really hard. It was the hardest call I've ever taken, the worst."

Roberto Reyes survived the subway crash but had to

have both his legs amputated. Lemuel Layda, who initially tried to free his compatriot Roberto, never rode the subway again.

The first fatal crash since the Toronto Transit Commission opened in 1954, it claimed three lives and shut down the Yonge-University-Spadina line for five days. Upwards of 200 of the 700 passengers in the two trains had suffered severe to minor abrasions, whiplash, and shock. A total of 135 commuters filed injury claims.

Though the TTC had experienced other mishaps, none of them had resulted in any fatalities. Compared to the rest of the world, the TTC has a good safety record. In Kaprun, Austria, 170 people were killed in a funicular subway accident after a fire on November 11, 2000. Since 1992, over 245 people have died in South Korea's Taegu subway. On November 1, 1918, more than 100 people died in a crash in Brooklyn when the driver took an S-curve, the most dangerous in the entire New York subway system, at more than 80 kilometres per hour.

A faulty trip arm caused the Toronto accident. It should have swung up and tripped or seized the train's brakes as the signal light turned red. Subway operator DeSantis, driver of the front train, sustained minor injuries. Robert Jeffery, the driver who slammed into the stationary car, suffered a broken collarbone, fractured ribs, and numerous abrasions. He left the Toronto Transit Commission and opened a coffee shop.

Chapter 7
Mel's Snow Emergency

With four centimetres of snow on the ground, Torontonians bustled around the city on the first official day of winter 1998, unhindered by the second lowest amount of the white stuff ever recorded in 155 years of record keeping. The temperature was above average, hovering around three degrees Celsius, so they scurried into the shops and malls looking for that perfect gift with Christmas only four days away.

A week later, a warm air mass moved from the Gulf of Mexico into southern Ontario. Local meteorologists predicted it would collide with an intense cold weather system heading down from the Yukon. But the next day, despite the –10 degree Celsius temperature, Torontonians paid little heed to the impending storm warning from Environment

Canada, ringing in the New Year until the wee hours.

On New Year's Day, a blizzard walloped the U.S. Midwest and veered toward Toronto. Snowflakes began to fall in the city around noon on January 2. Torontonians rushed out for shovels, salt, and antifreeze, and bought up all the snow blowers in town within a couple of hours. Video rentals increased by 25 percent with *There's Something About Mary* a favourite. That afternoon, 165 trucks fanned out across the city spreading sand and salt onto the streets as a precaution. Located in one of the most southerly regions of Canada, Toronto rarely experienced large snowfalls. In the 1980s, the annual snowfall had averaged about 120 centimetres.

By evening, the snowfall had intensified and 441 city snowplows began clearing the main thoroughfares. A car lost control on an icy street and slammed into a utility pole, leaving 400 residents in the suburb of Scarborough without electricity. Overnight, temperatures fell and the snow turned to freezing rain and back to snow again.

On Sunday, January 3, 1999, Torontonians woke up to a near record breaking 39 centimetres of snow. The temperature registered below freezing and winds gusted up to 70 kilometres per hour. Environment Canada had already issued a winter storm warning, advising people not to venture out in what could be hazardous whiteout conditions.

Like everyone else in the city, Toronto Mayor Mel Lastman woke up to mountains of snow burying cars, and snowdrifts choking the street and sidewalks outside his home. Mayor of the suburb of North York for 25 years before becoming Toronto's mayor, Lastman had never faced a predicament like a major snowstorm threatening to shut down the city.

With the merger in 1998 with North York, Etobicoke, Scarborough, York, and East York, Toronto had nearly quadrupled from 650,000 residents to 2.4 million. Now Lastman was in charge of the mega city. The storm could be the first real test for the snow removing operations of the newly amalgated metropolis. He realized the snow removal equipment was inadequate for such a colossal snowstorm. Toronto, after all, wasn't Montreal. The Quebec city had more than 3,000 vehicles to clear away nearly twice as much snow as Toronto received annually. With 5,100 kilometres of streets — almost equal to the distance from Toronto to Mexico — it had only a quarter of Montreal's snow removal equipment. The mayor felt he had no choice. Canada's largest city could not come to a standstill.

That afternoon, Mayor Lastman declared a three-day emergency snow removal plan, the first time in 16 years. This plan is activated when a significant amount of snow falls within an eight-hour period. "This is a real emergency," he declared as signs, and radio and television broadcasts warned motorists to avoid parking on major thoroughfares like University, Yonge, and Bloor. Police handed out tickets and towed away cars in violation of the ban.

Thankful the storm had not occurred on a weekday,

Torontonians ventured out to dig out their cars and clear their sidewalks of snow. They shovelled and shovelled, sweating and gasping from the physical exertion. Hundreds collapsed with chest pains and shortness of breath. Six of the city's 19 hospitals had to turn away emergency vehicles. By late that night, five deaths had resulted from snow shovelling.

And the problems kept mounting. A snowplow cut a gas line, forcing 50 people out of their homes. Impatient and reckless drivers drove too fast on slippery roads, lost control, and crashed into other vehicles. The police received hundreds of calls about fender benders. Frustrated passengers sat for hours on streetcars stuck in the snow. Bus drivers struggled up icy hills.

On one of the peak travel days of the year — the Sunday after New Year's Day — thousands of travellers returning from holiday visits or setting off to sunnier climes crammed the airport. Ground crews at Pearson International Airport struggled to keep the runways of Canada's busiest transfer hub free of snow. Air Canada cancelled 240 domestic and international flights, stranding 30,000 passengers and creating a domino effect across the country. People headed for the U.S. Midwest weren't going anywhere as airports there had shut down as well.

Throughout the airport's three terminals, tired and frustrated passengers milled around in long line-ups, sprawled on chairs or napped wherever they could. Others read newspapers or played cards and games. Some lined up at pay phones to call relatives or to reserve a room. But the hotels in Toronto were already booked solid. The line-ups for bathrooms snaked down the corridors. By nightfall, restaurants had nearly run out of food and drink.

Throughout Sunday night, city crews continued to work non-stop to clear the mountains of snow before the beginning of the work week.

Like thousands of other Torontonians on Monday morning, the day after the big dump, telephone repairman Brian Simpkins set off to work. Living near the north end of the city, he had a call to make downtown. "It took me a while to get my car out as I didn't have a shovel," he said. "My Ford Escort had front wheel drive so I rocked it back and forth a few times. Once I did that, I could take off no problem." A former Montrealer, he wasn't bothered all that much by the snow, but he admitted the city did not have enough equipment to handle the accumulation. Where he lived "the plow would go through and that was it," he said.

Other Torontonians weren't as nonchalant. Franco Marrallo had never seen it so bad in his 36 years on Markham Street, west of Bathurst. "The police put tickets on the cars but where are you supposed to put your car? On your head?" Retrieving their impounded cars, angry motorists lashed out at towing company employees as they forked out as much as $125 plus tax for parking on snow routes. The Canadian Automobile Association fielded 400 to 450 calls per hour from motorists stuck in the snow — three times the normal volume. The Toronto Transit Commission warned commuters that they faced continued delays unless snow removal was beefed up along major streetcar routes.

Traffic crawled along city streets. Despite the emergency edict, hundreds of abandoned cars still blocked nearly every highway ramp hindering motorists and hampering snow-clearing efforts. "The Morningside ramp on the 401 had nine vehicles left on it," said a dispatcher at the Ontario Provincial Police Communications Centre. "It took us over an hour to tow each one of them out and have that ramp plowed."

Deserted vehicles also blocked streetcar tracks along five downtown routes, leaving hundreds of irritated passengers and motorists sitting in traffic. A single car parked on the tracks backed up a dozen streetcars and detained commuters for close to an hour. Police and tow truck operators responded to call after call.

Still trying to get to his call, repairman Brian Simpkins encountered many buried vehicles lining the narrow streets of Little Italy and the Annex, west of downtown, and other older districts. "The snow plow came down the centre of the street and dumped a load of snow on the cars," he said. "They couldn't get out and a two-way street became one lane of traffic."

Underground commuters did not fare much better. Subway platforms swelled with waiting passengers as many left their cars at home. Pedestrians met with mountains of plowed snow that narrowed streets and forced them to climb over metre-high banks. Getting off a bus near Bay Street and Lake Shore Boulevard, Bing Roca and Cecilia Quitilen stepped into snow up to their waists. Another city commuter, Morgan Cotton, said, "I feel like I'm on a climbing expedition in the Himalayas," as he trudged along the unplowed sidewalks of Yonge Street. "You could break your neck trying to climb over the snow left by the plow."

Desperately needed help was provided by the Ontario government. After clearing highways, its work crews pitched in with their equipment to help with city snow removal. Public works also resurrected five infrequently used melting machines — last used six years earlier — and put them to work dissolving snow along main thoroughfares like Yonge and Bathurst Streets. Crews worked to widen the narrow streets despite fatigue and equipment breakdowns from the heavy use. Downtown residents complained about mammoth snow banks impeding garbage pickup and streets reduced to clogged one-way lanes. "It's pretty awful," a firefighter was reported saying, "We can get through — just."

Exhausted work crews toiled around the clock, removing 4,500 truckloads of snow and melting 38 kilometres of it. About half the city's crosswalks and transit stops remained unplowed, while mounds of uncleared snow narrowed high traffic thoroughfares. "There's so much snow that if you plow it from streets, you cover sidewalks," said Dave Kaufman, the city's senior director of transportation. "When you clear sidewalks, you put it back on the street."

Meanwhile, at Pearson International Airport, as operations tried to return to some normalcy, there were mishaps. An American Airlines flight slid into a snow bank upon arrival from New York and an Air Canada flight to Ottawa returned to Toronto after the pilot smelled smoke in the cockpit. Plagued by inadequate staff during the storm, Air Canada coped with a public relations disaster. Some travellers still paced the airport, waiting for flights out.

To add to the already precarious situation, only five days after the first storm, a second snow front began moving through the city on Friday, January 8 — right at rush hour.

On duty for seven straight days and working 16- to 20-hour shifts, exhausted crews moved from snow elimination to sanding and salting. Officials hoped the snow would not accumulate. All 1,800 city employees and contract workers had a day off scheduled over the next two days with half of them remaining on duty on each day. "It's getting to be a safety issue," Dave Kaufman said. "They're fried. They're frazzled."

Nine centimetres fell that night. Three days later on January 11, another 9.4 centimetres tumbled down. Over the next two days, 21 more unwelcome centimetres blew into town. On Wednesday morning, the temperature was −15 degrees Celsius with blowing snow and near zero visibility. Commuters stoically headed out to work only to find the transit systems crippled again by the snow. Frozen rail switches hampered Greater Toronto Transit Authority (GO

Transit) users to and from bedroom communities in the out-lying regions. The trains that did run experienced delays. One train from Mississauga arrived four-and-a-half hours late at downtown's Union Station.

For the first time in the system's history, the above ground sections of the subway were out of commission. Snow and ice clogged the third rail which supplies the power. The shutdown affected key sections of the Yonge-University-Spadina line, which ran north and south through the city transporting half a million commuters daily. Also closed was an outdoor stretch of track east of Woodbine on the Bloor-Danforth line.

"We'd never experienced snowstorms happening in such quick succession," said Gary Webster, general manager of operations at the Toronto Transit Commission. "Usually some sort of warm spell between them would melt the snow and we'd manage through with our normal snow fighting techniques."

Mayor Lastman held another emergency meeting with his officials at Command Headquarters at Toronto City Hall. He was in a tizzy again. Forecasters predicted another 15 to 25 centimetres of snow and extremely cold conditions over-night. The impending storm would be the fifth of the year and 1999 was barely two weeks old.

Toronto already resembled a ghost town. City and high-way driving remained treacherous and the public transpor-tation system was crippled. Schools shut down and children stayed home. Citizens were frustrated and short-tempered, all because of the white stuff, a natural winter occurrence in Canada.

The mayor wasted no time in declaring a second snow emergency that banned parking on major thoroughfares so snowplows could clear the streets. Then he placed a phone call to Art Eggleton, the federal minister of defence and a former mayor of Toronto. The minister listened sympathetically and then offered to send in the army.

When Lastman announced he had accepted military help, he said, "I'm petrified of what could happen. You come to a point where you can't push the snow back anymore. Then no cars can move. I have to have [the army] ready in case there's up to 25 centimetres of snow."

Canadian troops landed in Toronto on January 15. As Mother Nature dumped another 25 centimetres on the city, a contingent of more than 400 Royal Canadian Dragoons arrived. The unit previously serving in Somalia and Bosnia now had the assignment of shovelling snow in Canada's largest city. Their military equipment included snowshoes, shovels, and pickaxes, as well as 105 vehicles, ranging from armoured personnel carriers to trucks, snowmobiles, and four-wheel drive Jeeps. A reconnaissance team surveyed the damage. Four armoured Bison capable of hauling tanks and fallen hydro towers prowled the streets of Toronto. The all-terrain, eight-wheel-drive troop carriers could go over anything, claimed Brigadier-General Walt Holmes.

The media had a field day. Coverage of the army's invasion of Toronto was extensive. All the television stations held live broadcasts, interviewing soldiers as they shovelled out sidewalks and streetcar and bus stops. The diminutive Lastman became the target of editorial cartoons.

The rest of the country marvelled at the inability of Canada's largest city to cope with the snow. Hey Toronto, a lot of people joked, this is Canada. Get used to it.

The mayor of Revelstoke, Dr. Geoffrey Battersby, said his town of 8,500 had been amazed and amused by the collapse of Toronto after a total snowfall of about 110 centimetres. Revelstoke, Canada's snow capital in central British Columbia, had once recorded 2,446 centimetres in 1972 and averaged over 1,800 centimetres annually. The town's green grass on December 23 that year was covered by 174 centimetres of snow by noon on December 28. "We didn't have to shut the whole town," Dr. Battersby said.

Red-faced Torontonians were appalled by the mayor's actions. "The biggest annoyance during the snowstorms was the embarrassment caused by our mayor demanding military troops to save us from a few feet of snow," Steve Pitt said. "It was kind of funny but embarrassing for Toronto," said telephone repairman Brian Simpkins, who made it to his calls eventually. He blamed the mayor. "It was a Mel move. He was a real character so I wasn't surprised by it. But we were the brunt of a lot of good jokes for the rest of the country."

Mayor Lastman stood by his decision and remained

unapologetic. He ordered a street-by-street blitz to clear the city core of snow in two days so businesses could open on Monday, January 11, eight days after the first storm struck. Additional crews and equipment also poured in from Montreal and the Ontario cities of London, Bracebridge, and Ottawa. Prince Edward Island, Canada's smallest province, pitched in with 15 snow blowers and 29 dump trucks. After being shut down for five days, the transit system finally returned to full operation on Wednesday, January 13.

Altogether, the snowfall in January 1999 totalled 118.4 centimetres, the largest ever recorded, and cost the city $70 million to clean up — more than twice its annual budget for snow removal. Though almost a year's snowfall fell on the city in less than two weeks that year, Toronto has experienced larger one-day snowfalls. The previous record left 40 centimetres on the ground over a two-day period in December 1992. For the all-time record, a one-day blizzard on December 11, 1944, dumped nearly 49 centimetres, resulting in 13 deaths. Seven people died just trying to walk through the colossal snowdrifts.

Despite these earlier storms, the plight of Torontonians and soldiers shovelling snow was the year's top weather story in 1999 — much to the amusement of the rest of the country, which felt the "Florida" of Canada was long past due for a reality check.

Chapter 8
Invasion of the Insects

A swarm of tiny green bugs attacked Chris Darling as he stepped out of Toronto's Royal Ontario Museum (ROM) on August 2, 2001. They also coated the handlebars, tires, and frame of his bicycle. He bounced it on the sidewalk, trying to dislodge as many as possible, and wiped off the seat. Within a fraction of a second, they landed back on the bike as well as all over his body. A bug specialist — curator of insects at the Royal Ontario Museum — he knew insects well, but he couldn't identify these ones.

Chris pedalled home as fast as he could through the clouds and clouds of bugs billowing throughout the city on that smoggy, muggy afternoon. They clung to his damp skin and flew up his nostrils, and into his ears and mouth. He saw pedestrians furiously swatting the haze of insects as they tried to protect their faces under bandanas, sweaters, and jackets. They swarmed Tanya Takeuchi as soon as she walked out of her office building near Bay Street. "They were really annoying — just like a whole bunch of mosquitoes," she said. "They were flying into my face and clinging to my clothing."

Torontonians were flabbergasted. Dave Brennan dusted them off his suit and hailed a taxi. "It's like something out of a Stephen King film," he said. "I was walking past a park and there were so many I couldn't even see." As she walked along Richmond Street West brushing the insects off, Rosetta Powell said, "It's a plague coming down on the city. It's because we're too sinful." While some people used napkins and tissues to cover their mouths, Elana Freeman protected herself under an umbrella. "I thought it was going to rain today. But it rained bugs instead."

Torontonians had been sweltering through a record-breaking heat wave, hoping for some sort of relief. For nine straight days, temperatures soared over 30 degrees Celsius. Then when everyone thought the situation couldn't possibly get worse, the tiny bugs invaded the city. By mid-afternoon, hordes of flying insects sent children screaming and forced several public pools to close.

By 5 p.m., the Toronto public health office started receiving complaints. The phone lines rang incessantly throughout the evening. People were worried about catching some kind of disease from the bugs. Public health officials tried to reassure everyone that the insects posed no hazard, but advised residents to wear masks if they cycled or jogged.

Chris Darling arrived home from the ROM with bugs still crawling over his face, in his ears and hair, and all over his torso. "I had taken off my T-shirt and rolled it into a ball to capture the bugs inside," the bug specialist said. "I was curious to see what they were." So were numerous reporters who had left messages on his answering machine wanting to interview him about the infestation.

"In my 15 years in Toronto I had never encountered this kind of situation," Chris said. "It was like a detective story trying to figure out exactly what they were." He went to the bathroom and shook out his T-shirt in the tub. Bug after bug fell out. He gathered them up and examined them under a microscope.

The winged insect measured 0.16 centimetres in length, about the size of a speck of dust. It had a shiny black head and thorax with a dark green abdomen and a pair of black cornicles or tail-like appendages called tailpipes.

"Initially, all I knew was that they were aphids," Chris said. "I'm not an aphidologist or an aphid expert." He tried to contact his colleagues in Ottawa who were aphid experts, but in the middle of summer, everyone was away on vacation. So he photographed the pests to compare them to images he found on the Internet. It took some time to narrow down the species from the hundreds that exist.

The next day, the front pages of all the Toronto newspapers pictured people with shirts over their faces or covering their entire heads. Chris could describe the pests to reporters only as plant-eating aphids. He reassured them they posed no danger. The aphids did not bite or transmit plant-related diseases to people. Nor did he expect them to harm the city's gardens.

Chris presumed one of the hottest summers on record had caused the local species to multiply and spread out from the trees where they usually lived. Where they came from and why, he didn't know, but he predicted they would disappear by morning.

But the following evening, 20,115 fans gathered at Toronto's SkyDome to see the Blue Jays play the Baltimore Orioles. Also in attendance were trillions of aphids. In the stands, fans swatted at the bugs with their blue promotional bandanas and covered their heads with sweaters and jackets despite the 30-degree-Celsius heat. But it was no use, the aphids were as thick as a snowfall.

The players managed to complete two innings, rubbing their eyes and shaking their heads to keep the bugs off. "It was bad," said Blue Jays pitcher Kelvim Escobar. "Ears, eyes, nose. You have to breathe sometimes." During the third inning, home plate umpire Tim Welke asked for the SkyDome roof to be closed. Its vent-like flap sucked aphids out of the stadium but millions remained trapped inside.

Listening to the radio while driving home that night, Eric Richter, a sales representative for Sygenta Seed in London, Ontario, heard the news clip about swarms of insects flying around the SkyDome pestering players and fans. "I thought, Holy smokes! Then like Sherlock Holmes I put two and two together, and I just howled," he said. He called CBC radio and Chris Darling to tell them he knew what kind of bugs they were.

A month earlier, Eric Richter had looked forward to taking a couple of weeks off, but not without some concerns. Before leaving on vacation, he visited some customers in the heart of the agriculture belt of Southwestern Ontario — Middlesex County around London — about an hour-and-a-half west of Toronto. For his customers, it had already been a tough summer, one of the driest seasons on record for soybean growers. The extreme heat and sparse rain had hurt their crops. Growers faced the prospect of small yields and low prices for inferior grade soybeans.

As the farmers shared their concerns with him about the drought, Eric headed into the fields and walked down the rows to inspect the crop. The plants were obviously stunted from the lack of rain. Rather than measuring close to waist height, they languished around his knee. Eric crouched down and turned a soybean leaf over to check its underside. "I noticed several hundred bugs," said the self-described nature nut. "A little flag went up in my head."

In the early 1980s, Eric had interned at H.J. Heinz in

Leamington, Ontario. As part of his university studies, he analysed the impact of aphids on tomato plants. His research made him familiar with hundreds of the plant-eating species. So he was able to recognize the unusual leaf-munching pests on his clients' farms as soybean aphids or *Aphis glycines*.

The Asian species is native to China, Japan, and Indonesia. It initially entered the United States in 1999, though how the pesky creatures got there is unknown. Over the next two years, the pest devoured crops in state after state in the U.S. Midwest: Wisconsin, Illinois, Iowa, Michigan, and Minnesota.

Since he was preoccupied with going on vacation, "I didn't give it a lot of thought," Eric said, "other than to say to the growers that if the aphids got much worse we would certainly have to do something." A little more at ease, he went on vacation. When he returned toward the end of July, he paid another visit to his growers. "We walked into the fields and I noticed my pants got all sticky," he said.

Aphids feed through mouths shaped like tubes. They digest only a tenth of what they consume and expel the rest. The discharge called honeydew makes the leaves shiny and sticky, triggering a mould that turns plants black and rubbery with decay. Eric immediately realized the pests had substantially multiplied. "The aphids were everywhere," he said. "There were thousands and thousands and thousands, and they were killing the plants."

One of the soybeans farmers' worst fears had become

reality with the spread of the Asian aphid into Canada that year. Its arrival in Ontario threatened the province's largest field crop of more than 800,000 hectares and affected over three-quarters of the province's soybean growing area. First the severe heat and lack of rainfall, now a plague of insects threatened the livelihood of more than 25,000 Ontario farmers who grew 85 percent of Canada's soybeans. The annual crop was worth approximately $600 million.

"It was almost like the locust plague in Africa," Eric said. "The plants were so covered that if you tried to add another aphid, one would have to get off. The plants wilted by 10 o'clock in the morning because they were being sucked to death. An aphid sucks juice out of a plant like a mosquito sucks blood out of us." Colonies of several thousand aphids can populate one soybean leaf. They suck nutrients out of the leaves, stunting and yellowing the plants and reducing pod and seed production.

Eric wondered why the farmers weren't out spraying with pesticides. "If it was hurting the plant, I felt we should be spraying," he said. "But it was a politically sensitive topic. I was the lone voice in the forest." He checked with a few of his clients and found out the farmers disagreed about what to do because not much was known about the new pest.

Meanwhile, the aphids continued to multiply in the soybean fields. "Aphids multiply exponentially," Eric said. "They increase from one to two to four to eight under the right conditions."

Invasion of the Insects

As part of their complex life cycle, the sap-sucking aphids feed on leaves and produce generation after generation of wingless aphids until plants become too crowded. Then the females reproduce without mating and hatch aphids with wings in immense numbers. As part of their cycle, in late summer, these winged pests take flight to less populated soybean plants or in search of their alternate host, the buckthorn shrub, which grows in Ontario and is used mainly as windbreak.

On August 2, 2001, the prevailing winds drifted from the soybean fields of southwestern Ontario to the northeast. Riding the wind were hordes and hordes of weak but winged aphids. Although they were impossible to count, Eric roughly estimated that more than 150 trillion aphids blew into town, bugging Torontonians for the next couple of weeks.

Incredible photos of them swarming the city appeared in the newspapers. The devastation they inflicted also received media coverage.

"Now people in the city knew what the farmers were dealing with," Eric said. As to why so many ended up in the SkyDome, bug specialist Chris Darling could only guess, "They probably just collected there because it's a big bowl. In the late afternoon when it starts to cool down, they just fall out of the air."

Back in the fields, Eric had convinced some growers to spray the soybean crops on a trial basis in early August, but "it was almost too late as a lot of damage had already been done," he said. Rather than resorting to insecticides, the rest of the farmers waited for a more natural solution — ladybugs or lady beetles. The lady beetle, known as *Harmonia axyridis,* was intentionally introduced into the southern United States for aphid control. Imported in 1916 to attack aphids on peanut plants, the multicoloured Asian lady beetle is larger than the ladybug. The orange-and-black beetle eats 90 to 270 aphids a day, while its larvae consumes another 600 to 1,200 aphids. The species gradually had advanced north into Canada in 1994. "One day you go out in the field," Eric said, "and abracadabra the aphids are almost gone. What's left are these ladybugs."

After consuming what they could in the fields, the ladybugs looked for their favourite food elsewhere and followed it into towns and cities. They headed for the beaches and marinas, including the Island Yacht Club in Toronto Harbour. "There were tonnes of lady beetles around," Chris Darling said. Researchers estimated 1,000 times more beetles than during the previous year.

Later in the fall, after they had filled up on aphids, the lady beetles looked for warm nooks and crannies to winter in Toronto. They burrowed into the sunny, south facing walls of houses and attics. Toronto homeowners reported getting bitten, hard enough to draw blood, when they tried to evict the beetles. Though not considered a health hazard, they became another bug nightmare. Health officials advised owners to caulk cracks and crevices, and cover vents with screens.

The beetles didn't just eat the aphids. They were found to have a sweet tooth, especially for grapes. This new behaviour for lady beetles, Chris Darling speculated, may have been the result of a rapid depletion of food resources at the soybean fields. Another disaster erupted in the vineyards.

When Eric Richter went on a tour of Niagara vineyards that year, he asked the wine growers about the lady beetles. "Their faces just went white," he said. The wine growers had to submerge the harvested grapes in barrels of water and skim off the beetles that floated to the top. Despite these efforts, much to their chagrin, the brightly coloured pest got crushed and fermented with the grapes. A few lady beetles can ruin a batch of wine from the toxins in their bodies. "When you squish them, a blood-like secretion comes out," Eric said. "It's incredibly bitter, a wicked, wicked taste — even birds won't eat them."

Winemakers had to destroy 1.5 million litres of Ontario wine bottled in 2001 that had "the unmaskable hint of lady-bug," which caused them huge losses. Lady beetles continue to threaten 80 percent of the Ontario grapes grown to produce wine. Much to the displeasure of the soybean farmers, "the grape growers set up a research project on how to control the lady beetles," Eric said. "One thing they tried to do was restrict the acres of soybeans in the Niagara area." Fewer soybeans would mean fewer aphids and fewer lady beetles.

Since the lady beetles did not entirely solve the aphid problem in 2001, the soybean industry looked for other solutions. One was to set threshold guidelines for spraying insecticides on aphids. "When the aphids appear," Eric said, "we watch to see whether its predator, the lady beetle, increases at the same rate. If they do, they can hold the aphids in check and no spraying is done."

The driest summer in 54 years and the aphid infestation from mid-July to mid-August in 2001 cost the soybean farmers over $80 million while millions of Torontonians had been bothered and infuriated by the resulting insect invasions.

Toronto's SkyDome had been bugged on another occasion. On August 27, 1990, hordes of gnats or midges forced the roof to be shut. Can the city of Toronto expect more rural-urban problems in the future? The ROM's Chris Darling warned, "With global warming and the change in climate, there could be more pest problems than we have now."

Further Reading

Baird, Donal. *The Story of Firefighting in Canada.* Erin: The Boston Mills Press, 1986.

Collard, Edgar Andrew. *Passage to the Sea: The Story of Canada Steamship Lines.* Toronto: Doubleday Canada Limited, 1991.

Craig, John. *The Noronic is Burning.* Don Mills: General Publishing, 1976.

Gifford, Jim. *Hurricane Hazel: Canada's Storm of the Century.* Toronto: Dundurn Press, 2004.

Kennedy, Betty. *Hurricane Hazel.* Toronto: Macmillan of Canada, 1979.

Looker, Janet. *Disaster Canada.* Toronto: Lynx Images Inc., 2000.

Rasky, Frank. *Great Canadian Disasters.* Toronto: Longmans Green & Company, 1961.

Rawson, Nancy and Richard Tatton. *The Great Toronto Fire.* Erin: Boston Mills Press, 1984.

Schmidt, René. *Canadian Disasters.* Richmond Hill: Scholastic-TAB Publications Ltd., 1985.

Acknowledgments

The support of Pod colleague and writer Julie Gedeon in writing this book was immeasurable. In the short timeframe I gave myself to write this book, she motivated me daily and actively suggested changes to the text. A heartfelt thanks to her as well as to author Steve Pitt who generously passed along names of people to interview.

Especially to everyone I interviewed, a sincere and grateful thank you. You graciously gave your time to recall — what was for some — painful memories. I would also like to acknowledge the librarians at Pointe Claire Library, in Pointe Claire, Quebec, who diligently organized interlibrary loans of books and microfilms.

The Internet was an invaluable source as well as the archival newspaper files of the *Toronto Star,* the *Globe and Mail,* the now defunct *Montreal Star,* the *Gazette,* and *Le Journal de Montréal,* which provided some quotes and background information.

About the Author

Kathlyn Horibe writes and edits corporate communications and marketing texts for companies and associations. Her publishing credits include magazines and newspapers in Canada, the United States, Europe, and New Zealand. Prior to embarking upon a career as a writer, she held various management positions and lived in Toronto for two years.

Photo Credits

OTHER AMAZING STORIES®

These titles are available wherever you buy books. Visit our web site at **www.amazingstories.ca**

New **AMAZING STORIES®** titles are published every month.